WHERE DOES THE MARINE CORPS GO FROM HERE?

DATE DUE

Studies in Defense Policy
TITLES PUBLISHED

Naval Force Levels and Modernization: An Analysis of Shipbuilding Requirements
Arnold M. Kuzmack

Support Costs in the Defense Budget: The Submerged One-Third
Martin Binkin

The Changing Soviet Navy
Barry M. Blechman

Strategic Forces: Issues for the Mid-Seventies
Alton H. Quanbeck and Barry M. Blechman

U.S. Reserve Forces: The Problem of the Weekend Warrior
Martin Binkin

U.S. Force Structure in NATO: An Alternative
Richard D. Lawrence and Jeffrey Record

U.S. Tactical Air Power: Missions, Forces, and Costs
William D. White

U.S. Nuclear Weapons in Europe: Issues and Alternatives
Jeffrey Record with the assistance of Thomas I. Anderson

The Control of Naval Armaments: Prospects and Possibilities
Barry M. Blechman

Stresses in U.S.-Japanese Security Relations
Fred Greene

The Military Pay Muddle
Martin Binkin

Sizing Up the Soviet Army
Jeffrey Record

Modernizing the Strategic Bomber Force: Why and How
Alton H. Quanbeck and Archie L. Wood
with the assistance of Louisa Thoron

Where Does the Marine Corps Go from Here?
Martin Binkin and Jeffrey Record

MARTIN BINKIN *and* JEFFREY RECORD

WHERE DOES THE MARINE CORPS GO FROM HERE?

THE BROOKINGS INSTITUTION
Washington, D.C.

1775 Massachusetts Avenue, N.W., Washington, D.C. 20036

Library of Congress Cataloging in Publication Data:

Binkin, Martin, 1928–
Where does the Marine Corps go from here?
(Studies in defense policy)
Includes bibliographical references.
1. United States. Marine Corps. 2. United States
—Military policy. I. Record, Jeffrey, joint author.
II. Title. III. Series.
VE23.B5 359.9′6′0973 75-45068
ISBN 0-8157-0963-3

9 8 7 6 5 4 3 2 1

THE BROOKINGS INSTITUTION is an independent organization devoted to nonpartisan research, education, and publication in economics, government, foreign policy, and the social sciences generally. Its principal purposes are to aid in the development of sound public policies and to promote public understanding of issues of national importance.

The Institution was founded on December 8, 1927, to merge the activities of the Institute for Government Research, founded in 1916, the Institute of Economics, founded in 1922, and the Robert Brookings Graduate School of Economics and Government, founded in 1924.

The Board of Trustees is responsible for the general administration of the Institution, while the immediate direction of the policies, program, and staff is vested in the President, assisted by an advisory committee of the officers and staff. The by-laws of the Institution state: "It is the function of the Trustees to make possible the conduct of scientific research, and publication, under the most favorable conditions, and to safeguard the independence of the research staff in the pursuit of their studies and in the publication of the results of such studies. It is not a part of their function to determine, control, or influence the conduct of particular investigations or the conclusions reached."

The President bears final responsibility for the decision to publish a manuscript as a Brookings book. In reaching his judgment on the competence, accuracy, and objectivity of each study, the President is advised by the director of the appropriate research program and weighs the views of a panel of expert outside readers who report to him in confidence on the quality of the work. Publication of a work signifies that it is deemed a competent treatment worthy of public consideration but does not imply endorsement of conclusions or recommendations.

The Institution maintains its position of neutrality on issues of public policy in order to safeguard the intellectual freedom of the staff. Hence interpretations or conclusions in Brookings publications should be understood to be solely those of the authors and should not be attributed to the Institution, to its trustees, officers, or other staff members, or to the organizations that support its research.

FOREWORD

As the United States reassesses its national security policies in the wake of Vietnam, there is growing evidence that administration officials and legislators alike are beginning to look searchingly at one of this nation's most venerable institutions—the United States Marine Corps.

A major issue is whether the Marine Corps is appropriately geared to meet the most likely threats to U.S. national interests. Its emphasis on amphibious warfare needs to be reviewed in light of a changing international environment, which raises questions about the military and political viability of seaborne attacks on hostile beachheads. The ways in which that emphasis has shaped the Corps into a distinctively tailored light infantry force raises another issue: whether Marine ground units, short on firepower and cross-country mobility, could stand up to the sophisticated, heavily armored forces that can be fielded by the Soviet Union and its allies—and, if not, what should be done about it.

No less important is the role of Marine air power, which presently accounts for over half of all spending attributable to the Corps. The sharp contrast between its air force, which is designed for the most sophisticated kind of combat, and its infantry, whose fighting prowess still depends on the physical stamina of the rifleman, raises important questions about the future shape of Marine air power.

Finally, with the ending of the draft, the Marine Corps is finding the transition to an all-volunteer environment difficult. Whether or not its present size can be maintained without compromising the quality of its recruits needs to be assessed.

These questions are addressed in this study. The authors, Martin Binkin and Jeffrey Record, review the history and present organization of the Corps, analyze its prospects, define alternative responses to its problems, and outline the possible strategic and budgetary consequences of each.

This is the fourteenth of the series of Brookings Studies in Defense Policy. Like their predecessors, the authors have used only unclassified material. Their purpose is to contribute to knowledgeable discussion and professional judgment in a field that is increasingly the center of national debate.

Martin Binkin, a senior fellow in the Brookings Foreign Policy Studies program, is the author of several other studies in defense policy, among them *The Military Pay Muddle* (1975). Jeffrey Record, a former research associate in the same program, is also the author of other studies in defense policy, the most recent being *Sizing Up the Soviet Army* (1975).

The Brookings Institution wishes to thank General Wallace M. Greene, Jr. (USMC, Retired), and Robert W. Komer for their helpful comments. During the course of the study, the authors received useful data and assistance from numerous officials of the United States Marine Corps. They also benefited greatly from the comments of many on drafts of the manuscript, especially from those of John F. Ahearne, William R. Ball, Patrick J. Garvey, William M. Krulak, and Francis J. West, Jr. They are also grateful to their Brookings colleagues Robert Berman, Barry M. Blechman, James D. Farrell, Henry Owen, Jake W. Stewart, Robert G. Weinland, and Joseph A. Yager for valuable suggestions; to Barbara P. Haskins, who edited the manuscript; and to Ann M. Ziegler, who typed it.

The Institution acknowledges the assistance of the Ford Foundation, whose grant helps to support its work in defense studies. The views expressed herein are those of the authors and should not be ascribed to the persons who provided data or who commented on the manuscript, to the Ford Foundation, or to the trustees, officers, or other staff members of the Brookings Institution.

KERMIT GORDON
President

January 1976
Washington, D.C.

CONTENTS

Appendix

Tables

Figures

CHAPTER ONE

INTRODUCTION

November 1975 marked the two-hundredth anniversary of the United States Marine Corps. From the Barbary Coast to Belleau Wood to the sands of Iwo Jima to the jungles of Vietnam, the Marine Corps has forged a unique and impressive tradition of arms equaled by few other fighting forces in the world. Longstanding public celebration of the Corps has been evident in countless Hollywood epics, and in unshaken congressional support at times when the programs of other military services were under serious challenge. Its high public standing, relatively small size, and reputation for austerity have undoubtedly deflected many critics of U.S. defense policy from focusing on the Marine Corps.

There is growing evidence, however, that administration officials and legislators alike are beginning to take a hard look at the Corps. It is no secret that so-called force interdependence studies commissioned by Secretary of Defense James R. Schlesinger in early 1974 included an examination of the question: why a Marine Corps?

The secretary expressed his concern about continuing large-scale investment in amphibious warfare capabilities in his annual report to the Congress for fiscal 1976:

> [Our] amphibious forces are not cheap. Moreover, we are modernizing them not only so as to replace vessels of World War II vintage, but also so that all ships will have a 20-knot capability. These programs, their costs, and the delays that have attended their completion have raised questions about the need for an amphibious assault force which has not seen anything more demanding than essentially unopposed landings for over 20 years, and which would have grave difficulty in accomplishing its mission of over-the-beach and flanking operations in a high-threat environment.[1]

1. *Annual Defense Department Report, FY 1976 and FY 197T*, Report of Secretary of Defense James R. Schlesinger to the Congress on the FY 1976 and Transition Budgets, FY 1977 Authorization Request and FY 1976–1980 Defense Programs (February 5, 1975), p. III-26.

Moreover, the Senate Armed Services Committee, traditionally one of the staunchest protectors of the Marine Corps, is also apparently interested in reassessing the role, structure, and size of the Corps.[2]

A major issue is whether the United States Marine Corps (USMC), in partnership with Army ground forces, is appropriately structured to meet the most likely threats to U.S. national security. Despite experience since World War II, which has seen Marines fighting alongside the Army in Korea and Vietnam and despite current planning, which envisages Marines being involved in many different conflict situations (including war in Central Europe), the Corps remains organized, equipped, trained, and deployed *mainly* to conduct attacks from the sea.[3] This emphasis on the amphibious mission, which stems from a variety of military, political, and institutional factors, has shaped the Marine Corps into a distinctively tailored "light" infantry force—a force that in order to be readily deployable and adapted to helicopter and amphibious ship operations, conspicuously lacks armored fighting vehicles and heavy weapons. Such extreme specialization increasingly is being questioned as the military and political viability of amphibious operations declines, along with the U.S. Navy's capability to support such operations. Moreover, how useful Marine infantry forces—short in firepower and battlefield mobility—would be in nonamphibious contingencies against technologically sophisticated enemies is in serious doubt. In brief, the disadvantages of focusing on the amphibious mission could range from maintaining a larger Marine Corps than is warranted by national security considerations to inhibiting preparation of the Corps for more probable contingencies.

Another important issue is the proper role of Marine aviation, which presently accounts for over 55 percent of all spending attributable to the USMC.[4] Originally justified by the need for close air support during the as-

2. In its report on the fiscal 1976 defense authorization bill, the committee requested the commandant of the Marine Corps to undertake a study of force structure, mix of air and ground components, and manpower levels. See *Authorizing Appropriations for Fiscal Year 1976 and July–September 1976 Transition Period Authorization for Military Procurement, Research and Development, and Active Duty, Selected Reserve, and Civilian Personnel Strengths, and for Other Purposes*, S. Rept. 94-146, 94:1 (Government Printing Office, 1975), pp. 115–16.

3. *Fiscal Year 1976 and July–September 1976 Transition Period Authorization for Military Procurement, Research and Development, and Active Duty, Selected Reserve, and Civilian Personnel Strengths*, Hearing before the Senate Committee on Armed Services, 94:1 (GPO, 1975), pt. 3, p. 1442.

4. Compiled from data in United States Marine Corps, *FY 1975 United States Marine Corps Cost and Force Summary* (USMC, Headquarters, March 1975).

sault and consolidation phases of an amphibious landing, Marine aviation has now become a third air force, replete with a variety of sophisticated multipurpose aircraft that can perform many types of missions. By diversifying in this manner, the Corps may have denied its ground forces the cross-country mobility and firepower needed to meet the contingencies they are likely to face.

Finally, the Marine Corps is finding it even more difficult than the other services to attract sufficient qualified recruits in the all-volunteer environment. Indeed, it can be argued that attempts to maintain the USMC at its present size risk seriously lowered standards in the overall quality and discipline of Corps manpower, and by implication the USMC's effectiveness in carrying out any mission that might be assigned to it.

These and other issues are explored in this study, the purpose of which is to examine possible changes in USMC force structure and orientation. As background, chapter 2 reviews the origin and current foundations of amphibious warfare and its underlying doctrine; chapter 3 examines the structure, equipment, and costs of the Marine Corps today. The following three chapters analyze the major issues now confronting the Corps: the viability of the amphibious mission, the dominant questions pertaining to Marine air power, and the quality of manpower in the "all-volunteer" Marine Corps. Chapter 7 then presents alternative missions and structures that the United States Marine Corps might consider in the future and recommends changes that the authors feel should be undertaken in any event.

CHAPTER TWO

THE AMPHIBIOUS MISSION

The United States Marine Corps is a military force structured principally for amphibious operations, officially defined as "attack[s] launched from the sea by naval and landing forces embarked in ships or craft involving a landing on a hostile shore."[1] In preparation for this mission, Marine units are maintained in a high state of readiness; indeed, three or four battalion-sized landing teams are continually kept afloat aboard U.S. naval vessels for immediate employment in sudden or unexpected contingencies.

Origins

Since its establishment by a resolution of the Continental Congress in 1775, the United States Marine Corps (USMC) has performed a variety of missions. Some of them, such as sustained inland combat and counter-insurgency, have been carried out in conjunction with, and often under the overall command of, the Army; others, such as amphibious assault, represent tasks for which the USMC has been specially structured, and which in many cases it has performed independently of Army control.

During the Revolutionary War and throughout the nineteenth century, Marines were employed largely as naval infantry—as ship security units, boarding parties, and occasionally as expeditionary forces. Between 1798 and 1897, for instance, Marines participated in 128 combat engagements, seventy-nine (62 percent) of which may be classified as ship-to-ship operations, raids, or expeditions.[2] The small size of America's standing army in the 1800s often required Marines to serve as regular ground troops as well,

1. U.S. Marine Corps, *Doctrine for Amphibious Operations*, Landing Force Manual 01 (USMC, Headquarters, reprinted June 1970), p. 1-3.

2. Authors' calculations based on data appearing in William D. Parker, *A Concise History of the United States Marine Corps 1775–1969* (USMC, Historical Division Headquarters, 1970), pp. 133–35.

usually under Army command. For example, Marine units, along with sailors, state militiamen, civilians, and Army contingents, participated in the unsuccessful defense of Washington during the War of 1812. The chronic shortage of readily available trained manpower was also the primary reason for the extensive use of Marines as regular ground troops in the Mexican War and in World War I. In fact, Marines formed one-fifth of the first U.S. military contingent sent to France in 1917.[3] Augmented by reinforcements, these Marines were later established as a brigade of the Army's 2nd Infantry Division and participated in the battle of Chateau Thierry and in the Meuse-Argonne offensive.

The association of the USMC with amphibious warfare is a relatively recent phenomenon. Although the Corps has always been linked to the sea, and, more specifically, to naval operations, serious Marine interest in developing a capacity to assault defended beaches awakened only in the 1920s. This interest was in large part the result of two factors: first, the Corps' strong desire to establish for itself a unique mission that would preserve its independence, and second, the rise of Imperial Japan as the most likely future adversary of the United States.[4] The Army had rejected the amphibious assault mission, believing that the British disaster at Gallipoli in 1915 proved that attacks on hostile beachheads were technologically infeasible. The predominately insular nature of Japan's expanding empire made it essential to develop a capacity to seize and defend forward bases for naval operations, a task that required preparation for large-scale amphibious operations and that was willingly shouldered by the Marines.

The creation in 1933 of the Fleet Marine Forces and the establishment in 1934 of a suitable amphibious warfare doctrine with the USMC publication of the "Tentative Manual for Landing Operations" presaged the development of a sizable U.S. amphibious warfare capability. Unlike other Marine contingents, many of which during the interwar era were occupied with garrison duty and bandit suppression campaigns in Latin America, Fleet Marine Forces were "highly specialized amphibious assault troops" whose primary mission was "to serve with the fleet in the seizure and defense of advanced naval bases and in the conduct of such land operations as may be essential to the prosecution of a naval campaign."[5] As such, Fleet Marine

3. Ibid., p. 42.

4. Robert Debs Heinl, Jr., *Soldiers of the Sea: The United States Marine Corps, 1775–1962* (United States Naval Institute, 1962), pp. 253–57.

5. USMC, Marine Corps Development and Education Command, *Fleet Marine Force Organization 1973* (Quantico, Va.: USMC Education Center, 1973), p. 1.

Forces represented a remarkable if not revolutionary innovation, certainly in relation to traditional naval infantry.

U.S. preparation for amphibious warfare during the 1920s and 1930s was fully justified. The defeat of Japan in World War II hinged upon the success of a series of amphibious assaults conducted in the central Pacific that finally enabled the United States to bring to bear the full weight of its naval and air power against the Japanese home islands. U.S. Marine forces carried out most of these landings.[6] But they did not, conversely, participate in any of the great amphibious assaults in the European theater: the seaborne invasions of North Africa, Sicily, Salerno, Anzio, and Normandy were undertaken by Army units specially trained for such attacks.

World War II can justifiably be viewed as the golden age of amphibious warfare. The overthrow of America's principal adversaries—Germany, Italy, and Japan—depended in large part on a capacity to project power onto a hostile shore, a capability necessitated by the absence of friendly ground forces from the territory to be occupied. In contrast, America's major postwar adversaries—the USSR and the People's Republic of China—are autarkic, continental powers that not only are militarily independent of transoceanic lines of communication but also confront substantial ground forces of the United States and its allies deployed in neighboring countries. Indeed, since 1945 the United States has undertaken only one noteworthy amphibious assault—the September 1950 invasion at Inchon during the Korean War—and that assault was carried out by only six USMC battalions, equivalent to two-thirds of one division.

Uncontested or "administrative" landings, such as those undertaken in Lebanon in 1958 and in the Dominican Republic and Danang (South Vietnam) in 1965, have been more frequent. However, since World War II, Marine forces have been largely used as regular ground troops in sustained inland combat and not in amphibious operations. With the exception of the Inchon landing, Marine units in Korea fought in lengthy land campaigns under the direct control of U.S. Army corps commanders. Moreover, the few minor amphibious operations conducted by the Corps in Vietnam "appeared motivated less by tactical conditions than by a desire to establish precedent for use in post-war debate."[7]

6. Amphibious operations in the southwestern Pacific (the Solomons, New Guinea, and the Philippines) under the command of General Douglas MacArthur were conducted exclusively by U.S. Army forces.

7. F. J. West, Jr., "The Case for Amphibious Capability," *Marine Corps Gazette*, vol. 58 (October 1974), p. 22.

Current Foundations

The USMC remains a force structured mainly for amphibious warfare despite the declining incidence of this peculiar type of combat in the postwar era and the military and political constraints upon it that may be anticipated in the foreseeable future (see chapter 4). This focus is attributable to four main factors: the Marine Corps' statutory obligations under the National Security Act, the country's need for a quick-reaction capability, the likelihood of continuing U.S. force reductions overseas, and the Corps' desire to preserve its separate identity.

Statutory Obligation

The USMC has a statutory responsibility, embodied in the National Security Act of 1947, for the development of U.S. amphibious capabilities and doctrine. The key provisions of that act, as amended through 1973, assign the following organization and functions to the Corps:

> The Marine Corps, within the Department of the Navy, shall be so organized as to include not less than three combat divisions and three air wings, and such other land combat, aviation, and other services as may be organic therein. The Marine Corps shall be organized, trained, and equipped to provide fleet marine forces of combined arms, together with supporting air components, for service with the fleet in the seizure of defense of advanced naval bases and for the conduct of such land operations as may be essential to the prosecution of a naval campaign. In addition, the Marine Corps shall provide detachments and organizations for service on armed vessels of the Navy, shall provide security detachments for the protection of naval property at naval stations and bases, and shall perform such other duties as the President may direct. However, these additional duties may not detract from or interfere with the operations for which the Marine Corps is primarily organized.
>
> The Marine Corps shall develop, in coordination with the Army and Air Force, those phases of amphibious operations that pertain to the tactics, technique, and equipment used by landing forces.
>
> The Marine Corps is responsible, in accordance with integrated joint mobilization plans, for the expansion of peacetime components of the Marine Corps to meet the needs of war.[8]

A 1952 amendment to the National Security Act culminated an intense and often rancorous postwar debate within the Truman administration over

8. National Security Act of 1947, P.L. 80-253 (61 Stat. 495), as Amended through September 30, 1973 (GPO, 1973), pp. 16–17.

the role of the Marine Corps. Right after the war, the War Department, dominated by then Army Chief of Staff Dwight D. Eisenhower and U.S. Air Force Commander Carl Spaatz, viewed the USMC as an unwanted competitor with the Army for shrinking budgetary resources, and they both favored its drastic reduction to a 60,000-man force restricted exclusively to performing the "*waterborne* aspects of amphibious operations (duty as landing craft crews and beach labor parties)."[9]

In 1946 a bill was introduced in the Senate that would have empowered the secretary of defense to determine the size and missions of the USMC without congressional consent. It was defeated only by effective mobilization of congressional opposition on the part of USMC Commandant A. A. Vandegrift. Passage of the National Security Act in the following year was a major victory for the Marine Corps, because it reaffirmed the Corps' primary responsibility for the amphibious mission. But until 1952 there was no legislation regarding size so that the USMC was vulnerable to reductions that could effectively preclude it from carrying out that mission. Subsequent attempts were made by the cost-conscious Secretary of Defense Louis A. Johnson to cut the USMC. However, Marine Corps performance during the Korean War, coupled with growing congressional irritation at the administration's unremitting pressure to reduce the Corps, led to the passage in 1952 of the amendment to the National Security Act of 1947.[10] The future viability of the USMC as a sizable force of combined arms was thereby guaranteed. A minimum force level of three combat divisions and three air wings was stipulated, although the exact dimensions of each was left undetermined. The Marine Corps remains the only service with a statutorily mandated minimum active force structure.

U.S. Need for Quick-Reaction Capability

The ability to launch attacks on hostile territory from the sea contributes substantially to the U.S. capability to respond quickly to unforeseen contingencies around the world, a capacity deemed essential to the fulfillment of America's extensive treaty commitments abroad. The Corps' strong emphasis on readiness is justified on these grounds, as is the retention of units afloat. Whether amphibious forces are inherently more capable of responding rapidly to unforeseen contingencies than other types of forces is open to question, but many Marine experts are wedded to the notion that because

9. Heinl, *Soldiers of the Sea*, p. 515.
10. Parker, *A Concise History*, p. 87.

they are amphibious they are ready.[11] Indeed former USMC Commandant Robert E. Cushman, Jr., has characterized the Corps as "the Nation's versatile amphibious force-in-readiness."[12] The issue of USMC readiness is further complicated by the severe shortage of amphibious shipping, discussed in chapter 3, which precludes the sea movement of more than one of the USMC's three Marine Amphibious Forces at one time. Indeed, except for battalion landing teams already afloat, Marine ground units cannot be accurately characterized as "ready," in the sense of being able to respond rapidly to unexpected contingencies, because they are dependent mainly upon sealift for their strategic mobility. The pace at which they can be deployed is constrained by the time consumed in assembling sufficient ships, loading troops aboard, and moving to the target area (see pages 33 and 34). Thus the reaction time for a USMC force larger than two or three battalions is measurable in weeks and months rather than days.

In this regard the Marine Corps confronts a superior competitor in the U.S. Army's 82nd Airborne Division transported by the U.S. Air Force Military Airlift Command, which is expanding its capacity to convey forces both within and between potential theaters of military operations. Admittedly, the troops and supplies (especially heavy equipment and bulk items) that can be quickly deployed by air are limited and contingent upon the availability of secure terminal airfields, thus prohibiting airlift in contingencies requiring forcible entry. However, forces that are airlifted are bound to arrive in the crisis area much faster than forces dependent on sealift. On the other hand, there is nothing to preclude the airlift of Marine formations; in fact, Marine units often participate in airlift as well as parachute training exercises. The real issue is not whether the Marines are better configured than the Army for the quick-reaction mission—they are not—but rather under what circumstances should airlift be employed instead of sealift to fulfill that mission.

Declining U.S. Force Presence Overseas

A third argument for continued investment in amphibious forces rests upon the assumption that the continuing reduction, and in some cases out-

11. Marc A. Moore and Alfred J. Croft, Jr., "Roles and Missions: A Traditional View," *Marine Corps Gazette*, vol. 56 (June 1972); reprinted in Marine Corps Development and Education Command, "Marine Air Ground Task Forces Seminar," Annex D, Readings (Quantico, Va.: USMC, Education Center, 1973), p. AS-D-4-B-5.

12. "Statement before the Senate Armed Services Committee on Marine Corps Posture for FY 1976, 197T, and 1977" (USMC, Headquarters, February 1975; processed), p. 4.

right elimination, of U.S. bases and garrisons abroad places a premium on maintaining forces offshore. In the words of General Cushman, "as we reduce our overseas presence there will be an increasing reliance on our ability to project and sustain combat power from the seas."[13]

That overseas U.S. military deployments, particularly those in Asia, have been reduced in the post-Vietnam era—and will probably suffer further contraction—seems indisputable. However, there is little recognition in Marine Corps literature that one of the major consequences of the American debacle in Indochina will be sharply diminished prospects for any kind of direct U.S. ground combat intervention in foreign conflicts.[14] Indeed, a principal aim of the Nixon Doctrine—which heralded a new era of U.S. foreign policy following American intervention in Vietnam and whose underlying principles continue to guide America's Asian policy—was to ensure that "in some theaters the threshold of [U.S. military] involvement will be raised and in some instances involvement will be much more unlikely."[15] If so, then the requirement for amphibious assault forces, because they are inherently interventionary, is likely to be curtailed.

Institutional Self-Preservation

Finally, many Marines believe that preservation of the Corps' separate identity is contingent upon its ability to perform a unique mission. Marine Corps fears of being swallowed up by the Army are long-standing, and the Corps has deliberately avoided assuming tasks and responsibilities that might turn it into a second land army. Despite the way the Corps has been used since World War II, the USMC still views its monopoly of the amphibious assault mission as essential to its survival as an institution. Indeed, as discussed earlier, the Marines' adoption and development of the amphibious mission in the 1920s and 1930s was to no small extent attributable to the Army's rejection of it after World War I.

13. Quoted in Moore and Croft, "Roles and Missions: A Traditional View," p. AS-D-4-B-7.

14. Lawrence F. Snowden and Marshall N. Carter, "Sea-based Landing Force Operations: An Evolutionary Development," in U.S. Naval Institute, *Proceedings*, November 1972, p. 105. Similar views are expressed by George Fox, "The FMF and the Nixon Doctrine," *Marine Corps Gazette*, vol. 57 (March 1973), p. 34, and Arthur T. McDermott and others, "Seabasing: One Option," *Marine Corps Gazette*, vol. 57 (July 1973), p. 18.

15. Richard Nixon, *U.S. Foreign Policy for the 1970s: Building for Peace* (GPO, 1971), p. 14.

Doctrine

Amphibious operations are combined military operations of great complexity, requiring detailed and precise coordination of ground (assault), sea, and air forces. Present USMC amphibious doctrine is task oriented: the appropriate amount and combination of forces to be employed is determined solely by such objective factors as weather, terrain, and tidal patterns, and such subjective factors as the estimated size and capabilities of opposing forces anticipated on the beachhead and in surrounding areas.

The principal type of amphibious operation, and the one that commands the greatest USMC attention and resources, is the amphibious assault. Amphibious assault differs from other amphibious operations—withdrawals, demonstrations, raids, and special operations in support of assault—in that its goal is to emplace forces on a hostile shore. Indeed, it is preparation for assault, as opposed to other amphibious operations, that more than any other factor accounts for the Corps' peculiar structure and equipment.

The success of an amphibious assault is contingent upon the achievement of a "preponderance of force within the objective area."[16] This means that throughout the assault and the consolidation of forces ashore, there must be (1) naval supremacy against surface and subsurface enemy forces, (2) air superiority, and (3) clear preponderance over enemy land forces. Inability to meet even one of these requirements could jeopardize both the assault itself and the survival of forces that already have been landed. The Marine Corps apparently still harbors bitter memories of the Navy's abrupt departure from the landing area during the invasion of Guadalcanal in August 1942. Failure to clear surrounding islands of Japanese naval and air power compelled a premature withdrawal of naval forces supporting the assault, temporarily leaving the Marines "ashore without naval or air support and with only a portion of their assault supplies."[17]

Theoretically, there are five distinct phases of an amphibious assault operation, the first of which is *planning*. The responsibility for the coordination of plans submitted by various participants is assigned to the amphibious task force commander (almost always a ranking naval officer), who commands all ground, sea, and air forces during the initial phases of the assault. The planning phase also includes the assemblage and preparation of forces before their *embarkation*, the second stage of amphibious assault. *Rehearsal*

16. *Doctrine for Amphibious Operations*, p. 1-5.

17. James A. Donovan, Jr., *The United States Marine Corps* (Praeger, 1967), p. 39.

at sea of the planned operation constitutes the third phase and may be undertaken simultaneously with or followed by *movement* of the amphibious task force from ports of embarkation to the target area. The fifth and final phase is the *assault* itself, which is concluded by the "firm establishment of the landing force ashore."[18] Normally at some point during the assault phase control of the participating ground forces and supporting Marine Corps aircraft passes from the amphibious task force commander to the landing force commander.

The actual assault traditionally has been carried out by landing craft, amphibious tractors, and other amphibious craft. Since the 1950s, however, the Marine Corps has adopted a concept known as "vertical envelopment," which envisages reliance on helicopters deployed on troop ships as the principal—although certainly not the exclusive—means of transporting assault forces from ship to shore.

The advantages of vertical over waterborne assault are that it is swifter and permits the landing of forces behind enemy defenses in the immediate beachhead area. Its primary drawback is the helicopter's extreme vulnerability to ground fire, a weakness that was dramatically illustrated during the Marine assault on Tang Island following the Cambodian seizure of the U.S. merchant vessel *Mayaguez* in the Gulf of Thailand in the spring of 1975.

Of the eleven helicopters employed in the initial assault on Tang Island, five were quickly destroyed or disabled by small-arms and machine-gun fire. Moreover, evacuation of the Marines from Tang was delayed as the defenders, estimated at about 150 men, drove off helicopters trying to land on the island. Withdrawal became feasible only after two U.S. Navy destroyers and attack aircraft laid down a heavy suppressive fire.[19]

Continuing USMC procurement of attack helicopters to escort troop-carrying helicopters offers at best only a partial solution to this serious threat. Their possible contribution to the protection of a heliborne assault has not been recently tested in combat; contrary to Marine Corps doctrine, attack helicopters were not employed at Tang Island. In fact, the Marine assault force of about two hundred men, which had been flown into Thailand from Okinawa and the Philippines, was transported to Tang by the only U.S. helicopters immediately available: Thai-based U.S. Air Force helicopters whose pilots, though no strangers to combat, were not trained

18. *Doctrine for Amphibious Operations*, p. 1-6.

19. See reports by Drew Middleton, "Heavy Cambodian Fire Surprised the Marines," *New York Times*, May 16, 1975, and by John W. Finney, "Evacuation Ends Rescue Mission," *New York Times*, May 16, 1975.

in combined air assault operations. At the time of the assault a fully constituted battalion landing team complete with its assault and armed escort helicopters was en route to Tang aboard the U.S. carrier *Hancock* and was less than twenty-four hours away from the island. However, the President's decision to launch an immediate attack on Tang precluded its use.

Offshore supporting fire, designed to soften up beachhead defenses and to assist assault forces until their own artillery is landed, customarily has been provided by a combination of naval gunfire and carrier-based aircraft, usually the only friendly aircraft within range of the target area. However, the sharp decline of U.S. naval gunfire capabilities over the last decade (discussed in chapter 3) has placed the major burden on carrier-based aircraft during this critical phase.

The importance of rapidly amassing forces and supplies ashore once a beachhead has been securely established is paramount in current Marine Corps doctrine:

> The salient requirement of the amphibious operation is the necessity of building up combat power ashore from an initial zero capacity to full coordinated striking power as the attack drives toward its final objectives.[20]

Unfortunately, meeting this requirement necessitates the allocation of sizable numbers of troops, which otherwise could be "driving toward" their "final objectives," to the tasks of perimeter defense and unloading and distributing supplies. This pause to consolidate gives the enemy additional time to marshall its own forces in an attempt to halt expansion of the beachhead. The channeling of resources into the initial buildup at the expense of timely movement inland was a root cause of the British disaster at Gallipoli in 1915 and the near disaster that befell the U.S. landing at Anzio in 1944.

Current Marine proposals to overcome this handicap center on the concept of "seabase."[21] Under this concept a force ashore (less than the size of a division) would be supplied directly from ships at sea. Stockpiling of supplies on the beachhead and their subsequent transport overland to forward units would be avoided by airlifting supplies and troop replacements straight to those units from ships offshore. Thus the momentum of the assault would not be slowed by the need to build up sufficient forces in the landing area.

20. *Doctrine for Amphibious Operations*, p. 1-3.

21. For two differing views on the concept of seabase, see J. W. Hammond, Jr., "Seabase: The True Amphibious Operation," and Varle E. Ludwig, "Hazards of Seabase," *Marine Corps Gazette*, vol. 55 (August, 1971), and vol. 56 (February 1972), respectively; reprinted in USMC, Annex D, Readings, pp. AS-D-3-B-1, AS-D-3-G-1.

Critics of seabase argue that it would require the uninterrupted presence of a large supporting naval task force in the landing area as long as significant ground forces remained ashore. This requirement, by constraining task force mobility, would not only increase the ships' vulnerability to attack but also preclude their use elsewhere.

AMPHIBIOUS ASSAULT is perhaps the most intricate and difficult of all tactical military operations. Preparation for it requires both the creation of peculiar force structures and tactical doctrines, and the development of specialized and often costly weapons and equipment. Because the U.S. Marine Corps is the largest repository of amphibious warfare capabilities in the world, it is thus one of the world's most distinctively organized and equipped military forces.

CHAPTER THREE

THE MARINE CORPS TODAY

The National Security Act of 1947 as amended in 1952 established for the United States Marine Corps an active force level floor of three divisions and three air wings. Since then the Marines have enjoyed in Congress a political sanctuary that has been respected by administration officials and defense planners for over two decades. With the exception of the Vietnam buildup, during which the USMC was increased to four divisions, the three-division, three-wing structure has provided the principal basis for determining the size of the Corps. Manning levels have varied from a low of about 170,000 in 1960 to a high of close to 315,000 during the Vietnam era. Since the end of U.S. combat involvement in Southeast Asia, strengths have remained relatively constant at about 200,000 whereas the other military services have experienced modest manpower reductions. Table 3-1 shows that about 57 percent of all Marines are in units that together constitute the combat forces; another 24 percent are in noncombat support organizations, such as base operations, training, and logistic units; and the remaining 19 percent are in the "pipeline," either undergoing training or traveling between assignments.

Before discussing the major issues confronting the Marine Corps today in the following three chapters, the nature, composition, and cost of these Marine forces are reviewed below; so also is the budgetary and operational support provided by the Navy.

Marine Combat Forces

Marine combat forces consist of three major components: (1) infantry divisions composed of ground combat units and their attached support organizations; (2) a pool of supplementary specialized units, called "force

Table 3-1. Distribution of Manpower in the U.S. Marine Corps, Fiscal Year 1976

Category	*Number of people*
Combat forces	
Divisions	51,100
Air wings	37,000
Force troops	24,900
Subtotal	113,000
Support forces	
Base operating support	22,000
Training base (instructors, staff)	10,800
Command, logistics, and other support[a]	13,600
Subtotal	46,400
Troops in the pipeline	
Trainees and students	23,900
Transients, patients, and prisoners	13,000
Subtotal	36,900
Marine Corps, total	196,300

Source: Derived from Department of Defense, "Manpower Requirements Report for FY 1976" (February 1975; processed), p. XII-7.

a. "Other support" includes intelligence, research and development, and embassy security and major headquarters units.

troops," and (3) air wings consisting of fixed-wing aircraft, helicopters, and their respective support units.[1]

Combat Divisions

The fighting core of the division, shown in figure 3-1, consists of nine infantry battalions organized into three regiments. Each battalion is, in turn, composed of four rifle companies with 189 Marines apiece, organized into thirteen-man rifle squads—still regarded as the backbone of the Corps' fighting power. Mobility on the battlefield is by foot; electronic equipment, weapons, ammunition, and supplies are moved in small lightweight vehicles, most of them one-quarter-ton trucks and light weapons carriers. In addition to rifles and other individual weapons, battalion firepower includes a variety of direct fire assault and antitank weapons, such as machine guns, flame throwers, 66 mm and 3.5-inch rocket launchers, 60 mm and 81 mm mortars, and 106 mm recoilless rifles.

To upgrade Marine Corps antitank capabilities, rocket launchers and recoilless rifles are now being replaced by Dragon missiles. The Dragon is a

1. Unless otherwise identified, figures in this section are derived from Marine Corps Development Command, *Fleet Marine Force Organization 1973* (Quantico, Va.: USMC, Education Center, 1973), and updated using data supplied by USMC, Headquarters.

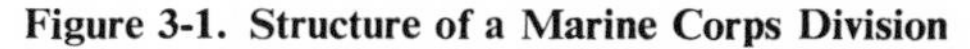

Figure 3-1. Structure of a Marine Corps Division

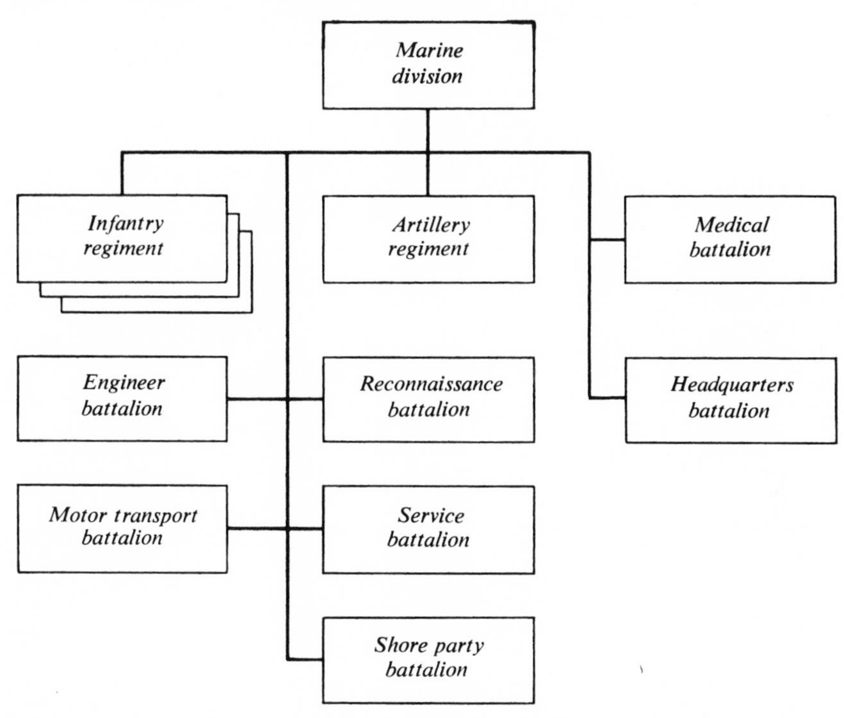

lightweight, man-portable weapon system designed for use against tanks and other hard-point targets such as emplaced weapons or fortifications. All Marine battalions are to be equipped with the Dragon by fiscal 1979.

An artillery regiment, composed of three artillery battalions (each consisting of three 105 mm batteries and one 155 mm battery) rounds out the available firepower within the division. The remaining divisional units, which play a supporting role, include a battalion-sized headquarters and engineering, medical service (supply and maintenance), and shore party units.

In sum, preoccupied with the amphibious assault mission, the Marines have ensured that virtually all elements within their divisions can be lifted by helicopters and are compatible with amphibious ships and landing craft. The Marine infantry division, with its emphasis on the individual rifleman and close-quarter, hand-to-hand combat tactics is, in fact, without a counterpart in either the U.S. or Soviet Armies (see table 3-2). Even the U.S. Army's few remaining fully active unmechanized infantry divisions are equipped with their own armor, heavy artillery, and armored personnel

Table 3-2. Comparison of Major Units and Selected Weapon Systems Organic to U.S. and Soviet Armored, Mechanized Infantry, and Infantry Divisions

	Armored divisions		*Mechanized infantry divisions*		*Nonmechanized infantry divisions*	
Item	*Soviet Union*[a]	*United States*[b]	*Soviet Union*[a]	*United States*[b]	*U.S. Army*[b]	*U.S. Marine Corps*
Personnel	9,500	16,500	12,000	16,300	14,600	17,800[c]
			Major units			
Infantry battalions	...	...	...	...	4–7	9
Mechanized battalions	3	4–5	9	5–6	0–2	...
Tank battalions	10	4–6	6	4–5	1–2	...
Artillery battalions	4	4	4	4	4	3
			Selected weapon systems			
Tanks[d]	325	216–324	255	216–270	54–108	...
Artillery						
Guns, heavy[e]	...	12	...	12	...	...
Guns, medium[f]	60	54	72	54	72	72
Antitank guided weapons	15[a]	...	54[a]	...	...	...
Dragon[g]		135–224[h]		162–256[h]	216	128
TOW[g]		90–134[h]		108–148[h]	144	...[i]

Sources: International Institute for Strategic Studies, *The Military Balance 1973–1974* (London: IISS, 1973), p. 80; Kenneth Hunt, *Defense with Fewer Men*, Part 2 of *The Alliance and Europe*, Adelphi Paper 98 (London: IISS, 1973), p. 24; and USMC, Marine Corps Development and Education Command, *Fleet Marine Force Organization 1973* (Quantico, Va.: USMC, Education Center, 1973), p. 14.

a. Figures represent the standard "Table of Organization and Equipment Strengths," listed in *The Military Balance* for full-strength (Category I) divisions. In reality these strengths vary from division to division.

b. Variable figures for battalions and tanks reflect actual differing composition of even the same type of division.

c. Includes U.S. Navy personnel assigned to the division.

d. The ranges shown for U.S. divisions reflect variations in the number of tank battalions.

e. Larger than 155 mm.

f. Between 105 mm and 155 mm.

g. Projected Dragon and TOW strengths upon completion of present program to replace rocket launchers and recoilless rifles with wire-guided antitank weapons. (The Dragon is a lightweight man-portable weapon system; the TOW is a crew-served missile system, heavier and with longer range than the Dragon.)

h. Higher figure applicable only to those U.S. divisions currently deployed in Europe or earmarked for contingencies arising in the European theater.

i. TOWs are to be retained outside Marine Corps divisions.

carriers. Indeed, the 82nd Airborne Division—the Army's lightest force—contains a battalion of small M-551 Sheridan tanks.

Force Troops

Additional firepower is available to Marine divisions from supporting units, called force troops, outside the division structure. These units contain six heavy artillery batteries—two equipped with self-propelled 8-inch howitzers and four armed with self-propelled 175 mm guns—and three 155 mm self-propelled artillery batteries. Three tank battalions, each with fifty-five tanks, are designed to provide close fire support for infantry units. M-48 and M-103 tanks, which have been in the Marine inventory for close to two decades, are now being replaced by tanks in the M-60 series. According to current plans, all Marine tank battalions should be equipped with M-60s by fiscal 1976. Marine infantry's dependence on foot mobility virtually precludes any use of tanks except to provide fire support for slow-moving ground formations. In contrast, the Army has organized its much greater tank strength to conduct high-speed, independent offensive thrusts accompanied by infantry aboard armored personnel carriers.[2] The Marines have recently formed antitank companies to enhance defense against armor; one is assigned to each tank battalion. Eventually these companies are to be armed with TOWs—a crew-served missile system, heavier and with a longer range than the Dragon, designed to destroy armored vehicles and fortified targets.

Also included in the force troops are three amphibious tractor battalions to transport men and equipment from assault ships to the beach, and to assist in subsequent operations ashore. These battalions are subdivided into nine companies, each with about fifty LVTP-7s (Landing Vehicle Tracked, Personnel). LVTP-7s can transport twenty-five men or 4.5 tons of stores at a speed of eight miles an hour on water and forty miles an hour on land. On land, however, because of its high profile, relatively large size, and thin armor, the LVTP-7 is inferior to the Army's M-113 armored personnel carrier—and very much inferior to the Mechanized Infantry Combat Vehicle scheduled for delivery to the Army in the late 1970s.

In addition, force troops provide other types of support needed to sustain combat divisions and, to a lesser extent, air wings. Included are communications, engineering, transportation, security, and reconnaissance units. The precise composition and employment of these supporting elements in a particular operation would be determined by specific require-

2. The U.S. Army's actual inventory of medium tanks (M-48 and M-60 series) was approximately 8,000 in fiscal 1975—2,000 units short of an authorized inventory of 10,000, and some 5,500 units short of an expanded authorized inventory of 13,500 requested in the FY 1976 defense budget. (*Annual Defense Department Report, FY 1976 and FY 197T*, Report of Secretary of Defense James R. Schlesinger to the Congress on the FY 1976 and Transition Budgets, FY 1977 Authorization Request and FY 1976–1980 Defense Programs [February 5, 1975], p. III-49.) Depending upon the number of tank battalions assigned to it, an army mechanized infantry division contains from 216 to 270 tanks and an armored division, 216 to 324, as shown in table 3-2. These figures dwarf the paltry 165 tanks mustered by all of the USMC's tank battalions.

ments peculiar to that operation; on average, there are about 8,000 Marines in force troop units that would typically support one division. Thus a Marine division and its supporting elements total about 26,000 men, or about 4,000 less than a typical Army division and its immediate supporting units.

Marine Air Wings

Unlike the Army, which must depend on the Air Force for most of its close air support, the Marine Corps has its own air arm—a special arrangement justified mainly by the close coordination critical to successful amphibious assault operations. Marine aviation includes 1,240 active "operating" aircraft performing a wide range of missions.[3] They include (1) offensive operations—close air support and interdiction; (2) air superiority, both offensive and defensive antiair warfare; (3) assault support operations, such as tactical airlift, air refueling, and casualty evacuations; and (4) aerial reconnaissance and electronic countermeasures.

In peacetime, Marine air units are organized formally into squadrons that can be transformed into task forces tailored to a particular contingency. The major squadrons, listed in table 3-3, are organized into three wings, each nominally consisting of three fighter and attack groups, one helicopter group, and their associated support units. The composition of a typical wing is shown in figure 3-2.

Aside from their diversity, the most striking feature of the Marine air wings is their size. Marine wings have twice as many fighter and attack aircraft as Air Force wings and provide a higher concentration of fire support to Marine ground combat units than the Air Force does to Army units. For example, the USMC could support each of its combat maneuver battalions with an average of fourteen fighter and attack aircraft whereas the Air Force, even if fully committed to the close air support mission, could provide an average of only ten fighter and attack aircraft for each Army combat maneuver battalion. This rough measure may be oversimplified but it illustrates the relative abundance of air support that Marine ground forces enjoy—an advantage that helps to offset their comparative lack of firepower on the ground. Indeed, their strong air support has enabled the Marines to

3. In addition, the Marine Corps possesses 214 "nonoperating" aircraft: those in the maintenance pipeline and those considered inactive. An additional 220 aircraft are assigned to the Marine Corps Reserve. (United States Navy, "Historical Budget Data" [March 1975; processed], pp. 12–13.)

Table 3-3. Marine Corps Active Tactical Aviation Forces, Fiscal Year 1976

Type of aircraft	*Unit equipment aircraft per squadron*[a]	*Number of squadrons*
Fighter and attack		
F-4	12	12
A-4	16	5
A-6	12	5
AV-8	20	3
Reconnaissance and electronic warfare		
RF-4	21	1
EA-6	21	1
OV-10	12	3
Helicopter		
AH-1	18	3
UH-1	21	5
CH-46	18	8
CH-53	18	6

Source: Derived from *Fiscal Year 1976 and July–September 1976 Transition Period Authorization for Military Procurement, Research and Development, and Active Duty, Selected Reserve, and Civilian Personnel Strengths*, Hearing before the Senate Committee on Armed Services, 94:1 (GPO, 1975), pt. 9, p. 4748.

a. Unit equipment (or UE) strength is the number of aircraft that would be deployed in wartime. The unit, however, usually possesses a larger inventory for training and to offset those in maintenance. Moreover, additional aircraft are maintained to offset possible attrition.

engage successfully in a number of operations that would have otherwise been considered impracticable.

Nowhere is the Marine Corps' emphasis on amphibious operations more apparent than in the composition of its aviation forces. The Corps' roster of aircraft conspicuously reflects strong naval influence; without exception, Marine combat aircraft are compatible with shipboard operations and with few exceptions, they exemplify a common procurement policy for Navy and Marine aircraft prevailing since World War II. The composition of Marine aviation forces is described in detail in the appendix.

Marine Reserve Forces

The Marine Corps Reserve fulfills three principal missions: it provides elements that might be lacking in the active division-wing team; it furnishes a full division-wing team in support of operations in the event of general war; and it fleshes out the support establishment in the event of general mobilization.

The organized reserve consists of about 35,000 billets and is structured, trained, and equipped along lines similar to the active-duty division-wing team. Currently, it has the equivalent of one division, one aircraft wing, and combat and service support units, which together constitute the Fourth Ma-

Figure 3-2. Structure of a Marine Corps Aircraft Wing

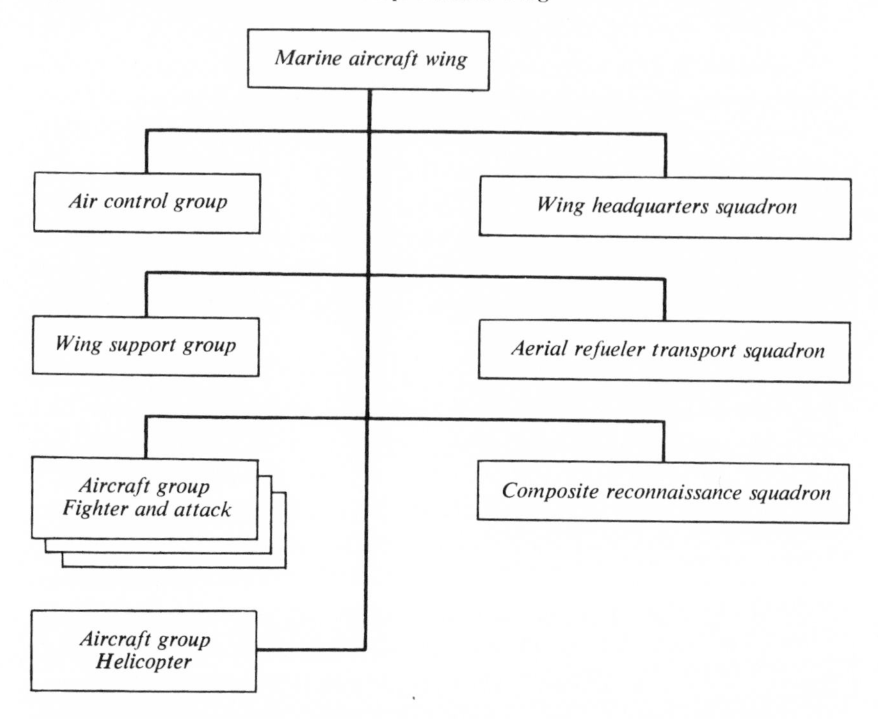

rine Amphibious Force. The Fourth Marine Division is headquartered at Camp Pendleton, California, and the reserve air wing—the Fourth Marine Aircraft Wing—is headquartered in New Orleans. The wing is composed mainly of aircraft inherited from the active forces; indeed, the pace of modernization in the reserves is almost entirely dependent on the rate at which the active forces are modernized.

According to Marine sources, the Fourth Division could not be deployed as a division earlier than two months—but more likely not until five months—after mobilization, whereas the air wing could probably be deployed within two months.[4] There is low probability therefore that the Fourth Marine Amphibious Force would be called upon to operate autonomously. Reservists used as individual fillers or smaller reserve units such as rifle companies could probably be deployed much earlier.

4. Testimony of Lieutenant General Samuel Jaskilka, *Fiscal Year 1976 and July–September 1976 Transition Period Authorization for Military Procurement, Research and Development, and Active Duty, Selected Reserve and Civilian Personnel Strengths*, Hearing before the Senate Committee on Armed Services, 94:1 (GPO, 1975), pt. 3, p. 1409.

The Task Force Concept

While division and wing counts are the most common means of expressing force levels, the "task force concept"—tailoring organizations for specific missions—has become a hallmark of Marine Corps planning. Obviously, many combinations of integrated ground and air combat units could be assembled with the available building blocks. For planning purposes, however, three general task forces—expressed in fractional equivalents of one division and wing team—are used: the Marine Amphibious Force (MAF), the Marine Amphibious Brigade (MAB), and the Marine Amphibious Unit (MAU).

The Marine Amphibious Force, as shown in table 3-4, is the largest of the task force organizations nominally consisting of the division-wing team described above. In peacetime, combat elements at the division-wing level are organized under three Marine Amphibious Force headquarters; each MAF includes a ground combat division, an air wing, and associated force troops. Two MAFs—the First at Camp Pendleton, California, and the Third in Okinawa—are under the jurisdiction of the Fleet Marine Forces, Pacific; the Second MAF, at Camp Lejeune, North Carolina, is under the control of the Fleet Marine Force, Atlantic. When committed to combat, however, a MAF could conceivably vary in size from about one-half of a division-wing team to a force composed of two divisions and two wings with appropriate support. A legacy of World War II amphibious assault campaigns, MAF-sized operations appear to attract little attention in Marine Corps planning today; even training exercises of that magnitude are rare, the most recent having been conducted in 1972. The last assault even approaching this size was the Inchon landing in 1950.

The Marine Amphibious Brigade is a smaller task force normally composed of one infantry regiment and one aircraft group. For operational planning purposes, however, a task force of from two-ninths to five-ninths of a division-wing team would be called a MAB. Also designed for low- to mid-intensity conflicts, the MAB could be deployed afloat for extended periods, although none of the currently deployed units are that large. The last amphibious operation of this size was an unopposed landing at Chu Lai, Vietnam, in 1965.

The Marine Amphibious Unit normally consists of a battalion landing team (BLT) supported by a composite helicopter squadron. The smallest of the task organizations, MAUs are routinely forward deployed; currently, three are continuously maintained afloat—one in the Mediterranean

Table 3-4. Composition of Marine Corps Task Force Organizations

Type of Marine task force	*Fraction of a division-wing team*	*Typical ground combat element*	*Aviation combat element*	*Scope of operations*	*Nominal manpower strength*
Marine Amphibious Unit (MAU)	$\frac{1}{9}$	Battalion landing team (BLT)	Composite helicopter squadron	Limited; immediate reaction to crises; light unsupported opposition; routinely deployed forward	2,200 Marines 200 Navy
Marine Amphibious Brigade (MAB)	from $\frac{2}{9}$ up to $\frac{5}{9}$	Regimental landing team	Marine aircraft group	Low- to mid-intensity conflict situations	For $\frac{3}{9}$ division-wing team: 13,600 Marines 2,000 Navy
Marine Amphibious Force (MAF)	from $\frac{5}{9}$ up to 2	Marine division	Marine aircraft wing	Wide range of combat operations of any intensity and in any geographic environment	For 1 division-wing team: 44,700 Marines 2,300 Navy

Source: Based on unpublished data provided by United States Marine Corps, Headquarters (1975).

Table 3-5. U.S. Navy Amphibious Ships, 1975[a]

Designation	*Type of ship*	*Number*
LCC	Amphibious Command	2
LPH	Amphibious Assault	7
LKA	Amphibious Cargo	6
LPA	Amphibious Transport	2
LPD	Amphibious Transport Docks	14
LSD	Dock Landing Ships	13
LST	Tank Landing Ships	20
Total		64

Source: Based on data appearing in John E. Moore, ed., *Jane's Fghting Ships, 1974–75* (Jane's Yearbooks, 1974).

a. Excludes the *La Salle*, an LPD in use as a flagship of the Middle East force, which could be pressed into use for amphibious operations if necessary.

and two in the Pacific—and one is deployed intermittently in the Caribbean.[5] In addition, a reinforced company is garrisoned at Guantanamo Bay, Cuba. These units are designed mainly to signal American interest in a region and for immediate reaction in crisis situations. It was a forward-deployed MAU in Puerto Rico, for example, that first went ashore in the Dominican Republic in 1965.

Naval Support

To fulfill its amphibious role the Corps relies on the U.S. Navy for shipping to lift Marine ground forces and for fire support during the initial phases of an assault operation.

The Amphibious Fleet

The Navy presently operates sixty-four amphibious lift ships. This fleet, which is one of the most modern in the Navy (most of the ships were built after 1960), consists of the variety of vessels listed in table 3-5. All are capable of sustained speeds of 20 knots. They are organized into Amphibious Task Units (ATUs) usually containing from three to five ships each. When deployed in peacetime, these ATUs and their Marine components are sometimes referred to as Amphibious Ready Groups (ARGs).

Typically, the only Amphibious Ready Groups routinely constituted are those carrying the Marine forces deployed in the Mediterranean, the Pacific, and the Caribbean. The number and type of ships in an ARG varies;

5. Depending upon the availability of amphibious shipping, a MAU is deployed in the Caribbean for six-week periods, after which it returns to its home base at Camp Lejeune for about ten weeks.

a formation capable of lifting a Marine Amphibious Unit might consist of the following: an amphibious transport dock (LPD), a dock landing ship (LSD), an amphibious assault ship (LPH), and two tank landing ships (LST).

The current inventory of amphibious vessels is sufficient to sustain the continuous forward deployment of three battalion landing teams (one of which is unaccompanied by its helicopter group because of a shortage of deck space), and the intermittent deployment of a fourth battalion landing team, also without helicopters.

Over the long term, according to the Department of Defense, "[the] objective is to provide a sufficient number of modern 20-knot ships to transport simultaneously the assault elements of 1⅓ Marine Amphibious Forces (MAFs), that is, 1⅓ Marine division-wing teams together with their unit equipment (excluding fixed-wing aircraft, which are transported on attack carriers or flown to the theater) and initial stocks of supplies."[6] This force, it is maintained, could support an amphibious assault by one division in a major combat theater (along the NATO flanks, for example) and at the same time cope with a minor crisis elsewhere. It would be necessary, however, to transfer ships, say, from the Pacific to the Atlantic to support such a division-sized assault in Europe.

The capability to lift 1⅓ MAFs is expected to be attained with a fleet of five large assault ships (LHAs), scheduled to enter the fleet between fiscal 1976 and fiscal 1979. These ships will be capable of performing missions now requiring several different types of smaller vessels. Together with two of the new *Newport*-class tank landing ships, one LHA will be able to carry and land a full battalion landing team, its weapons, vehicles, tanks, and artillery. With five LHAs, the fleet should be capable of continuously maintaining four BLTs deployed afloat.

Naval Gunfire Support

Amphibious doctrine assigns to naval gunfire and tactical air the task of softening up beach defenses until artillery can be moved ashore, after which they would protect beach flanks and reinforce artillery fire. During World War II, the Navy possessed a large fleet of ships capable of providing fire support for amphibious operations, including battleships with 12- to 16-inch guns and cruisers with 6- to 8-inch guns. Because most of those vessels

6. *Annual Department of Defense Report, FY 1975*, Report of the Secretary of Defense James R. Schlesinger to the Congress on the FY 1975 Defense Budget and FY 1975–1979 Defense Program (March 1974), p. 138.

were decommissioned shortly after the end of the war, fire support during the Korean War was limited; naval gunfire at Inchon, for example, was provided by two heavy cruisers, two light cruisers, eight destroyers, and four "medium landing ships-rocket" (LSMRs), which had been commissioned at the end of World War II. All battleships and heavy cruisers have since been retired; the largest naval guns presently available in the active fleet to support amphibious operations are of 5-inch caliber.[7] Even the newest *Spruance*-class destroyers entering the fleet during the remainder of this decade, which are designed mainly for antisubmarine warfare, mount only two 5-inch guns apiece.

On the other hand, a new, lightweight major caliber (8-inch) gun is in the late stages of development by the Navy and could possibly be available by the end of the decade. Indeed, the *Spruance*-class ships were designed so that this system could be added later. However, the Department of Defense has yet to request funds for the modification.

Under current plans, in fact, future amphibious assault operations would have to be conducted without the naval gunfire support that has previously been available. Lamenting this fact, a former marine commandant expressed his concern to Congress in 1973:

> During amphibious assault operations, until our organic artillery is established ashore, naval gunfire provides the only surface, all-weather, long-range fire support available to the landing force. At present, only the [heavy cruiser] *Newport News* is capable of providing major caliber support, and her continuation in the active fleet is tenuous. There is also a programmed reduction of ships with smaller caliber guns which would be dedicated to naval gunfire support missions.[8]

Just how much fire support the Marines would like to see in the fleet has not been divulged. The World War II rule of thumb for assaulting beaches defended by the Japanese and Germans was one destroyer (with four to six 5-inch guns) supporting each battalion, one heavy cruiser (with nine 8-inch and sixteen 5-inch guns) for each regiment, and one battleship (with eight to

7. Between 1964 and 1974, the total number of gun barrels—3-inch or larger—mounted on active naval vessels declined by 70 percent (from 1,294 to 385), reducing total salvo weight by 82 percent (from 7.1 to 1.3 short tons). This trend reflects the attitude among many Navy officials that needed fire support will be provided by carrier-based aviation, which they argue can provide accurate and high-volume ordnance delivery. This is analogous to the general trend in the Department of Defense to invest in Air Force tactical aircraft instead of Army artillery. (Calculations based on data in relevant issues of *Jane's Fighting Ships* [Jane's Yearbooks].)

8. "Testimony by General Robert E. Cushman, Jr.," *Department of Defense Appropriations for 1974*, Hearings before a Subcommittee of the House Committee on Appropriations, 93:1 (GPO, 1973), pt. 2, p. 268. The *Newport News* was decommissioned in June 1975.

twelve 14- or 16-inch guns) for each division.[9] The implications for future amphibious operations of reduced levels of support available are discussed in chapter 4.

Costs

The Marines enjoy a long-standing reputation as the most austere of the U.S. fighting forces. Exhibiting a comparatively high "teeth-to-tail" (combat-to-support) ratio and generally shunning the comforts and conveniences sought by the other services, the Corps comes across unmistakably as a national security bargain.

This impression has been a significant factor in the relations of the Marine Corps with Congress, as illustrated by the views of the Senate Armed Services Committee in 1972—the year in which it recommended substantial reductions in military manpower in the other services:

> In the opinion of the Committee, the Marine Corps continues to exemplify the lean, austere fighting force that today is dictated by the high cost of manpower. The Marine Corps has done an outstanding job in maintaining an efficient fighting unit . . .[10]

The efficiency with which the Marine Corps operates, however, is difficult to assess, in part owing to the lack of understanding about how much the Corps really costs.

On the surface, the Corps consumes a small part of defense resources; for fiscal 1976, its $2.7 billion budget request was less than 3 percent of the total defense budget. This figure, however, does not reflect most of the costs of Marine aviation, which are included in the Navy budget; research and development, procurement, operating, maintenance, and training costs associated with Marine aviation forces are budgeted in Navy accounts. In addition, the costs of several expensive services (for example, medical care, construction, and supply support) are not included, because they are also provided for the Marine Corps by the Navy.

When the appropriate Navy costs are allocated to the Marine Corps, the full outlay in fiscal 1975—the most recent year for which detailed data are available—was approximately $3.8 billion, as shown in table 3-6, which

9. Brooke Nihart, "With Reputation and Spirit Intact," *Sea Power* (April 1972); reprinted in Marine Corps Development and Education Command, Annex D, Readings, p. AS-D-4-H-1.

10. *Authorizing Appropriations for Fiscal Year 1973 for Military Procurement, Research and Development, Construction Authorization for the Safeguard ABM, and Active Duty and Selected Reserve Strength, and for Other Purposes*, S. Rept. 92-962, 93:2 (GPO, 1972), p. 137.

Table 3-6. Estimated Full Cost of the U.S. Marine Corps
Total obligational authority in millions of 1975 dollars

Force element	*Direct costs*[a]	*Indirect costs*[b]	*Total cost*	
			Amount	*Percent*
Division forces	926	755	1,681	44
Aviation forces	1,329	819	2,148	56
Helicopter	235	189	424	11
Fixed wing	1,094	630	1,724	45
Marine Corps, total	2,255	1,574	3,829	...

Source: Estimates derived from data in USMC, Office of the Deputy Chief of Staff, Requirements, and Programs, "FY-75 United States Marine Corps, Cost and Force Summary" (USMC, May 1975; processed).
a. Includes costs associated with combat units, their organic support, and direct support costs not associated with a particular combat unit but clearly related to the overall mission. (For example, the costs of operating Camp Lejeune are direct costs of division forces.)
b. Includes costs associated with units or functions that are not easily allocated to a single specific mission. (For example, a portion of the cost of operating Headquarters, U.S. Marine Corps, is allocated to each mission.)

was substantially higher than the $2.5 billion Marine Corps budget. If, in addition, the costs of naval amphibious shipping are imputed, the Corps' full annual cost in 1975 would have approached $7 billion.[11]

One striking feature indicated in table 3-5 is the large share of total resources committed to Marine aviation—particularly to the fighter and attack mission—a consequence, in part, of the more expensive support tail characteristic of advanced aviation technology. Given the present course, moreover, the aviation element of the air and ground team is bound to consume a growing proportion of total resources. Such a trend has been emphasized by the steady movement toward more sophisticated and more expensive aircraft (see the appendix). Marine wings are to be equipped with new fighter aircraft; their attack aircraft fleet is being modernized; and plans to develop what will undoubtedly be a more costly successor to the relatively new VSTOL aircraft have been announced. It is estimated that such modernization programs together will cost an average of about $600 million a year for the remainder of the seventies. Furthermore, as these increasingly complicated aircraft enter the inventory, greater demands will be placed on the support establishment. The larger number of Marines needed to maintain the more sophisticated airborne systems will require recruitment of those with higher technical skills and could mean fewer, or less qualified, infantrymen. In short, the prospects for relief from the financial demands being imposed on the defense budget by Marine aviation are dim.

11. According to the Department of Defense, the annual cost of naval amphibious forces (amphibious ships and escorts) is about $3 billion. (See *Department of Defense Authorization for Appropriations for Fiscal Year 1976*, Hearings before the House Armed Services Committee, 94:1 [GPO, 1975], pt. 1, p. 1825.)

CHAPTER FOUR

PREPARATION FOR AMPHIBIOUS WARFARE: HOW MUCH IS ENOUGH?

A principal issue confronting the United States Marine Corps today is the future viability of the amphibious mission. Is the continuing preoccupation of the Marine Corps with amphibious warfare founded upon a realistic appraisal of future U.S. requirements for such a capability? To what extent will amphibious assault remain a technologically feasible military operation? Military, technological, and political considerations govern the future of such operations. Admittedly, these considerations affect nonamphibious as well as amphibious forces. Indeed, some bear directly on the very willingness of the United States to resort to military force. In this regard, it is important to keep in mind that amphibious forces are inherently structured for offensive operations and, in the case of the United States Marine Corps, have been more closely associated than the other services with American military intervention abroad.

Military and Technological Constraints

There are at least four military and technological obstacles that constrain future USMC exercise of its amphibious warfare capabilities: the continental character of most potential U.S. adversaries, the presence of U.S. or friendly forces overseas, the advent of precision-guided munitions, and the U.S. Navy's declining support of the amphibious mission.

The Continental Adversary

Unlike Imperial Japan and Fascist Italy, few of America's postwar adversaries have been dependent upon the maintenance of oceanic lines of communication for their ability to wage war. The USSR and the People's

Republic of China, the two most prominent potential adversaries of the United States, are large comparatively autarkic continental powers; while amphibious assaults along coasts controlled by either country cannot be ruled out, such operations could only marginally influence the outcome of conflict with either nation. That outcome would be determined largely by sustained inland combat campaigns or by the use of nuclear weapons.

Presence of U.S. and Allied Forces Overseas

It is generally the absence of friendly forces ashore in areas that need to be taken and held (such as the Japanese-held Solomon Islands in 1942–43 or Nazi-occupied Western Europe in 1944) that generates a need for large amphibious assault capabilities. However, in Europe and in a number of Asian countries there are already sizable U.S. military contingents already ashore. The presence of these garrisons, together with the substantial allied forces listed in table 4-1, greatly reduces the likelihood of the United States ever again having to employ large amphibious forces, as it was compelled to do at Normandy, to "fight its way back" into these countries. (This is discussed later in relation to specific regions.)

Advent of Precision-Guided Munitions

How technologically viable are amphibious operations in the years ahead? As demonstrated in the 1973 October War between Israel and the Arab States, and during the last stages of direct U.S. combat involvement in Indochina, precision-guided munitions (PGMs) degrade the survivability of armored fighting vehicles and aircraft while heightening that of dispersed infantry. Although USMC ground forces possess comparatively few tanks or other fighting vehicles, and thus are distinctly labor- rather than capital-intensive, Marines are completely dependent upon amphibious landing craft and helicopters for transport during the assault phase of an amphibious operation. During the assault both landing craft and helicopters are likely to be very exposed to hostile fire. Moreover, the presence offshore of sizable naval forces in support of an amphibious assault offers attractive targets for weapons "whose probability of making a direct hit at full range upon a tank, ship, radar, bridge, or airplane (according to its type) is greater than a half."[1] Indeed, a major tactical implication of PGMs

1. James F. Digby, "Precision-Guided Munitions: Capabilities and Consequences," P-5257 (RAND Corporation, June 1974; processed), p. 2.

Table 4-1. Size of U.S. and Allied Ground Forces[a] in the European and Asian and Pacific Areas, 1975
Thousands of men

Country	*U.S. forces*	*Allied regular forces*	*Allied reserve forces*	*Allied paramilitary forces*[c]	*Total*
Europe[b]					
Belgium	...	65.4	8.0	15.0	88.4
Britain	...	182.7	300.0	55.3	538.0
Denmark	...	21.5	69.5	50.0	141.0
France	...	331.5	400.0	70.0	801.5
Federal Republic of Germany	...	340.0	518.0	20.0	878.0
Greece	...	121.0	230.0	99.0	450.0
Italy	...	308.2	550.0	80.0	938.2
Netherlands	...	77.8	300.0	7.7	385.5
Norway	...	17.7	135.0	60.0	212.7
Turkey	...	365.0	750.0	75.0	1,190.0
Europe, total	200.0	1,830.8	3,260.5	532.0	5,823.3[e]
Asia/Pacific					
Australia	...	31.2	20.2	...	51.4
Japan	...	154.0	39.0	...	193.0
New Zealand	...	5.6	2.6	3.0	11.2
Philippines	...	35.0	218.0	34.9	287.9
South Korea	...	580.0	1,000.0	2,000.0	3,580.0
Taiwan	...	375.0	815.0	175.0	1,365.0
Thailand	...	139.0	200.0	63.0	402.0
Asia/Pacific, total	55.0[d]	1,319.8	2,294.8	2,275.9	5,945.5[e]

Source: International Institute for Strategic Studies, *The Military Balance 1974–1975* (London: IISS, 1974).
a. Including marine and naval infantry.
b. Excluding the forces of Luxembourg and the European-based forces of Portugal and Canada.
c. Encompassing militia, gendarmerie, border police, territorial defense, and homeguard forces.
d. Including U.S. Army forces in Korea, Hawaii, and USMC forces forward deployed in the Pacific.
e. Total includes U.S. forces.

is that "it will become much less desirable to concentrate a great deal of military value in one place."[2]

The helicopter, to which present Marine Corps doctrine assigns the principal role of transporting assault units to and beyond the beachhead, is especially vulnerable to ground fire, to say nothing of PGMs. Its comparative slowness, lack of armor protection, and inability to fly at higher altitudes render the helicopter an attractive if not easy victim of PGMs. This extreme vulnerability was a major "lesson" drawn from the October War[3]

2. Ibid., p. 6.

3. See, for example, Kenneth Hunt, "The Military Lessons," *Survival*, vol. 16 (January–February 1974), p. 4; Kenneth S. Brown, "The Yom Kippur War," *Military Review*, vol. 54 (March 1974), p. 25; and Martin van Creveld, *Military Lessons of the Yom Kippur War: Historical Perspectives* (Sage Publications, 1975).

and was markedly evident in the Marine assault on Tang Island in May 1975, following Cambodian seizure of the American merchant ship *Mayaguez*.

The USMC has responded to this problem by procuring fast AH-1J Sea Cobra attack helicopters to escort troop-carrying helicopters and to suppress hostile ground fire (see appendix). Escorts undoubtedly would enhance the survivability of heliborne assault forces, although whether they would justify continued reliance on the helicopter as the primary means of transporting attacking Marine ground troops is open to question.

PGMs obviously raise the intensity of combat and in so doing directly threaten the potential success of amphibious assault operations, which have always fared better in low-intensity conflicts. Indeed, the proliferation of new and more effective PGMs among third world armies over the coming decade could blur the distinction between high- and low-intensity combat—a distinction of cardinal importance in extant USMC amphibious warfare doctrine. The simplicity and inexpensiveness of many PGMs, as well as the comparatively little training necessary to operate them, make PGMs ideal weapons for the heretofore technologically unsophisticated infantries of Asia, the traditional arena of major USMC amphibious operations.

Declining Naval Support

Many Marines, citing declining amphibious shipping levels and naval gunfire support capabilities, claim that the Navy is insensitive to Marine Corps amphibious warfare requirements. Such a claim is not without foundation.

During the Kennedy and early Johnson years the Navy advocated full funding of the forces it considered necessary for its entire spectrum of missions, which since the late 1960s, in the Navy's order of priority, have been: (1) strategic deterrence, (2) sea control, (3) projection of power ashore, and (4) naval presence. Under later fixed budget concepts, competition between the various Navy programs and missions has become more intense and highly visible. Not surprisingly, the Navy has focused on amphibious shipping as a prime candidate for cuts.[4]

The paucity of amphibious shipping is perhaps the greatest material constraint upon amphibious operations. The continued maintenance of three Marine Amphibious Forces (MAFs) makes little sense, because globally

4. The Marine Corps itself must compete for Department of the Navy resources; it is no secret that the annual struggle to divide the Navy Department's budget between Navy "blue dollars" and Marine Corps "green dollars" is often less than amiable.

scattered amphibious shipping is sufficient to transport only one MAF. This shipping deficiency reduces by two-thirds the amount of U.S. amphibious warfare capabilities that could be employed at one time. The level of amphibious shipping is thus not surprisingly a major bone of contention between the Marine Corps and the U.S. Navy. Nor is the realization of a projected capacity to lift one and one-third MAFs by fiscal 1977 likely to deflate the issue. A minimum of forty-five days still will be required to assemble, load, and transport to the target area a MAF-sized amphibious task force. To lift one MAF, amphibious shipping would have to be transferred from the Pacific to the Atlantic (or vice versa).

On the other hand, since 1945 the USMC has never conducted an amphibious assault, an administrative landing, or even a peacetime training exercise involving more than one MAF. And with the growing political constraints on direct U.S. military intervention abroad discussed below, it is difficult to foresee an amphibious assault contingency requiring the use of more than one Marine division-wing team. So the need for expanded amphibious lift is not clear.

As for naval gunfire support capability, while its decline is indisputable, it is not at all apparent that the success of amphibious assault operations is contingent on the availability of large quantities of naval gunfire. Nor is it obvious that a significant portion of that gunfire support must be delivered by guns of 8-inch caliber or larger. This would depend, in large part, on the character of beach defenses to be overcome.

Naval gunfire is more accurate than air-delivered munitions and is possible under all weather conditions, and even after the initial bombardment has clouded the target with dust, smoke, and debris. But the ability to find mobile targets for naval guns before assault forces establish themselves ashore is likely to depend on the weather-constrained aerial observation of forward air controllers. Moreover, the issue of comparative accuracies between naval and air bombardment is fast becoming moot with the proliferation of "smart" bombs.

Historically, the effectiveness of naval gunfire in reducing coastal defenses has been limited. During the later stages of the Pacific campaign in World War II, for example, many Japanese beachhead fortifications and bunker systems survived naval and air attack largely because their precise position was unknown, or because they were located well underground and thus undetectable from the air. It is improbable that such formidable coastal defenses, which in World War II often took years to construct, will be built any more. And this further reduces the requirement for naval gunfire in excess of the 5-inch guns now available.

Although naval gunfire can be used in almost any kind of weather, an amphibious assault probably would not be launched in conditions sufficiently inclement to preclude the use of carrier aircraft. Poor visibility, strong winds, and rough seas would, in fact, not only reduce the guns' effectiveness by inhibiting aerial detection of targets but also jeopardize the very success of the assault by hindering the use of helicopters and landing craft. The largest amphibious assault in history—the invasion of Normandy scheduled for June 5, 1944—was postponed for a full day because of unusually bad weather, although the weather on June 6 (D-Day) was still very severe. Naval gunfire played an important part in the success of the operation. The key question for the future, however, is whether hostile beach defenses will require prolonged and accurate bombardment.

Domestic Political Constraints

Whether amphibious forces will be needed or feasible in the broad context of U.S. national security planning is one set of issues. Another—even broader—relates to the political decisionmaking process: the anticipated reactions at home to any form of direct U.S. military intervention overseas and the likelihood and scale of contingencies arising abroad that could be met most effectively with amphibious forces.

There is growing public disenchantment with military ventures overseas, particularly those involving the use of ground troops. In addition, with deepening absorption in domestic problems, the importance attached to foreign affairs by the American public during the 1950s and 1960s has sharply declined over the past several years, and there are no indications that this attitude is likely to change significantly in the foreseeable future. The bitter aftertaste of U.S. immersion in the Vietnam quagmire, an increasingly troubled economy, and declining confidence in political institutions as effective engines of social and economic reform are but a few of the many factors that have stimulated a public focus on domestic concerns unparalleled in intensity since the 1930s.

This shift in attention is indisputable. Virtually every public opinion poll taken on the subject since 1968 confirms it.[5] The principal consequence of

5. For example, a national canvass conducted in the spring of 1974 by the Institute for International Social Research revealed that the following problems, ranked in order of importance, were the highest among the public's concerns: (1) The rise in prices and the cost of living; (2) the amount of violence in American life; (3) crime in this country; (4) corruption and lawbreaking on the part of government officials; (5) the problem of drug addicts and narcotic drugs; (6) insuring that Americans in general, including the

such growing public attention to internal problems is a lower threshold of public tolerance for the direct exercise of U.S. military power overseas and thus a diminishing willingness to "send in the Marines." Disenchantment with U.S. military "adventures" abroad is already manifest in continuing congressional pressure to reduce U.S. military garrisons overseas, to cut foreign military and economic assistance, to block U.S. entanglement in Angola, and in the passage of the War Powers Act of 1973.

Regional Implications

Against this background it may be useful to examine briefly politico-military prospects for U.S. amphibious operations in specific regions.

UNLIKELY CONTINGENCIES. Latin America, Africa, the Indian Ocean (excluding the Persian Gulf), and Southeast Asia are regions in which it is unlikely that U.S. ground troops will be directly engaged in combat.

In Latin America, we can conceive no plausible scenario that would require landing major U.S. combat forces anywhere in South America (outside the Caribbean), given the vigor of local nationalism and the large U.S. stake in maintaining a viable political and economic relationship with its hemispheric neighbors. Even an intervention in the Caribbean to protect U.S. nationals or U.S. installations—for example, in the Canal Zone—would in all probability assume the character of an administrative landing.[6]

Africa is also a region in which chances for sizable U.S. military intervention on land are remote, even to thwart renewed Soviet meddling in lo-

---

elderly, get adequate medical and health care; (7) protecting consumers against misleading advertising, dangerous products, and unsafe food and drugs; and (8) cleaning up waterways and reducing water pollution. (William Watts and Lloyd A. Free, eds., *State of the Nation 1974* [Harper Colophon, 1974], pp. 20–21.)

Of a total of thirty subjects identified by respondents as major national issues, only eight were related to foreign affairs, all of them falling in the lower half of the spectrum of importance. In sharp contrast are the results of a similar poll taken by the institute in 1964, which showed that the top five major national concerns of the American public were: (1) keeping the country out of war; (2) combating world communism; (3) keeping military defense forces strong; (4) controlling the use of nuclear weapons; and (5) maintaining respect for the United States in other countries. (William Watts and Lloyd A. Free, eds., *State of the Nation* [Universe Books, 1973], p. 34.)

In the 1974 poll, "keeping our military and defense forces strong" was in the seventeenth place, lagging behind such issues as the energy shortage, air pollution, unemployment, and garbage and solid waste collection and disposal.

6. Approximately 7,000 U.S. Army personnel, including the 2,500 men of the 193rd Infantry Brigade, are currently stationed in the Canal Zone.

cal strife, such as that taking place in Angola in late 1975. U.S. combat troops have never been used in sub-Saharan Africa. If U.S. military forces can play any useful role in the racial and other confrontations that can be foreseen on that continent, they will probably be limited to providing logistical support to United Nations peacekeeping forces brought in to separate the belligerents. And such U.N. contingents would almost certainly be made up of troops from the smaller powers.

In the Indian Ocean, excluding approaches to the Persian Gulf, it is very difficult to foresee a plausible occasion for U.S. intervention. There may well be further fighting on the Indian subcontinent, but it is not clear that important U.S. interests will be involved or that U.S. forces could play any useful role in bringing conflict to an end. Any use of American force in this region almost certainly would be limited to air and naval operations.

In Southeast Asia the case for U.S. amphibious operations is not evident in the wake of Vietnam. A clear consensus has emerged in the United States against any American role in future Southeast Asia ground fighting, based on the judgment that the United States has no vital interest in the area. The most that can be foreseen in this region is perhaps a small administrative landing to evacuate U.S. nationals.

In sum, the growing disposition of the American public and government is to reject a U.S. security role in most of the developing world. The Vietnam experience has convinced Americans that U.S. national interests in these areas are not sufficient to warrant military intervention, short of a direct attack on the few U.S. forces remaining in those regions. This view seems unlikely to change.

POSSIBLE CONTINGENCIES. To the extent that there remains a substantial interest in a U.S. security role abroad, it focuses increasingly on the main industrial areas and the Middle East.

In Japan's defense, important U.S. interests are involved, as they are in fulfilling our commitments—so long as they are maintained—to the defense of the Republic of Korea and to Taiwan, because of the impact of developments in these regions on Japan. But here, again, the presence of allied and U.S. forces ashore limits the need for amphibious operations. Even if substantial cuts are made in U.S. ground troops in Korea (now about 34,000), there would remain 580,000 and 1 million men, respectively, in the active and reserve forces of the South Korean Army. Japan also has sizable conventional air and ground forces, as does Taiwan. Although the territory of each of these countries is already in friendly hands, limited amphibious operations might prove useful—particularly in Korea—in facilitating the progress of friendly forces along the main battle front. Such was the intention of the Inchon landing in 1950.

Similarly, in Europe some amphibious operations can be envisaged. For example, Norway's defense in a war in central Europe that threatened to spill over to NATO's northern flank would require landings at key points along the coast in order to bolster that country's small armed forces. And effective resistance to a similar expansion of the conflict into NATO's southern flank might depend upon the timely arrival of seaborne reinforcements. Yet such operations in the context of a general war in Europe would be—as they were in World War II—of only secondary importance, since the outcome of the conflict ultimately would be decided in NATO's crucial Central Region.[7] Indeed, the demand for resources in NATO Center (the Federal Republic of Germany, excluding Schleswig-Holstein) could strip U.S. capabilities earmarked for flank contingencies.[8]

Moreover, amphibious assaults on beachheads controlled by Soviet ground forces or within range of Soviet land-based aviation would be infeasible if not suicidal. The prospect of attaining local air superiority to protect supporting carrier task forces and suppress beachhead defenses is slim, and it is not surprising that some U.S. Navy officials appear reluctant to commit surface forces under such conditions.[9] Thus, although scenarios involving amphibious *assaults* along either NATO flank are viewed by many Marines as the Corps' most important potential contribution to the defense of Europe, sizable amphibious operations along the flanks probably would be confined to *administrative* landings designed to deter Soviet expansion of hostilities, rather than assaults aimed at dislodging Soviet forces already in place.

In the Middle East, amphibious assaults designed to reduce Arab pressure

7. The Central Region of the North Atlantic Treaty Organization includes the Benelux countries and the Federal Republic of Germany (excluding Schleswig-Holstein).

8. In the fall of 1975, 1,500 Marines participated in "Autumn Forge," a NATO training exercise conducted in northern Germany. The exercise, which marked the first time since World War I that USMC forces had been deployed in the Central Region, took place in the Hannover area and was devoid of any simulated amphibious assault operations.

9. According to Admiral Thomas H. Moorer, former chairman of the Joint Chiefs of Staff, and Admiral Elmo R. Zumwalt, Jr., former chief of naval operations, it would be "dangerous for the United States . . . to deploy, in a bilateral confrontation with the Soviet Union in the Eastern Mediterranean, its fleet because the odds are that the fleet would be defeated in a conventional war." "Meet the Press," June 30, 1974 (NBC transcript, p. 6). The threat presumably would be greater in the Norwegian Sea, which is even closer to deployed Soviet land-based aviation than is the Eastern Mediterranean.

on beleaguered Israeli forces in some future war in that region cannot be prudently discounted, nor can the possibility of contested landings designed to extract endangered American citizens.

Indeed, in the politically volatile Middle East, a combination of important U.S. interests, an absence of reliable indigenous forces allied to the United States, and lengthy littorals conducive to seaborne assault all suggest a more credible prospect for amphibious operations. And the cutting edge of any U.S. military intervention in that region dictated by a sudden or unexpected contingency almost certainly would be a composite of Marine and U.S. Army airborne contingents. Of all possible military contingencies it is the prospect of U.S. action in the Middle East that is most often cited as justification for undiminished preparation for amphibious warfare.

Yet the U.S. Marine Corps (and, for that matter, the U.S. Army's 82nd Airborne Division) is not optimally configured to confront the likely opponents of the United States in another war between the Arab states and Israel. Marine units are essentially light infantry formations best suited for relatively low-intensity combat in topography that precludes or severely constrains the effective use of armored fighting vehicles. Yet in a conflict against Egypt, Syria, or Iraq, Marines would be engaging highly mobile, heavily armored ground forces possessing great firepower in terrain often tailormade for armored warfare. The availability of carrier-based aviation and sophisticated antitank weapons such as the TOW and Dragon[10] certainly would enhance Marine antiarmor capabilities, although Marine forces would still lack the necessary degree of firepower (tanks) and mobility (armored personnel carriers) *on the ground* that are essential in dealing effectively with tank and mechanized infantry attacks. This judgment is supported by a Defense Department assessment of the October War:

> Our continuing analysis of the recent Middle East war has convinced us that the tank is still the single most important land forces weapons system wherever armored forces can be utilized effectively. This is true even in the European context, where NATO's overall strategy is primarily defensive and the Warsaw Pact strategy is primarily offensive. While we believe that modern antitank weapons

10. In fiscal 1976 and 1977 the USMC plans to procure some 3,700 TOW and 15,564 Dragon missiles. The Dragon missile is a lightweight man-portable weapon system and the TOW is heavier and with longer range, served by a crew. A TOW missile company will be added to each of the Corps' three active and one reserve tank battalions. Dragons will be assigned to infantry battalions down as far as the squad level. (*Annual Defense Department Report, FY 1976 and FY 197T*, Report of Secretary of Defense James R. Schlesinger to the Congress on the FY 1976 and Transition Budgets, FY 1977 Authorization Request and FY 1976–1980 Defense Programs [February 5, 1975], pp. III-42, 43, 55.)

fired from the air as well as the ground can provide an effective counter to the modern tank, it should be recognized that these weapons are useful primarily in a defensive role. The ground-based versions do not have the protection, mobility and versatility of the tank, particularly when used in the local counter-offensive role; the air-launched versions, although highly mobile, are still weather-limited.[11]

In the Persian Gulf, the prospects for U.S. intervention are more remote, although the armed forces of potential U.S. adversaries are smaller and much less sophisticated than those of Arab states bordering Israel. However, the Gulf states are substantially upgrading their military capabilities. A good example is Saudi Arabia, whose vast oil fields were recently cited as a potential objective of U.S. military intervention in the area, should such action be deemed necessary to halt the debilitating effects of a future oil embargo imposed upon the West by the Organization of Petroleum Exporting Countries.[12] Yet this particular U.S. military option is becoming steadily less attractive because Saudi Arabia's traditionally small and relatively primitive armed forces are being expanded and modernized. The Riyadh government has contracted to buy first-line French arms worth some $825 million dollars; they include 200 AMX-30 main battle tanks (to add to an existing inventory of 150 AMX-30s), 250 armored cars, and large numbers of surface-to-air and antitank missiles. Weapons and equipment, including improved Hawk missiles and some sixty F-5E and F-5F fighter aircraft, worth another $1.01 billion, are being procured from the United States. Moreover, the Department of Defense (through the California-based Vinnell Corporation) has undertaken a $77 million contract to train the Saudi National Guard in, among other things, the techniques of sabotaging oil fields.

Stronger local resistance would be only one of the risks attending U.S. intervention in the Persian Gulf. Others include the threat of Soviet air and naval counterintervention, which would compel supporting U.S. carrier task forces to stay out of the Gulf; the virtual impossibility of achieving a degree of surprise sufficient to preclude Arab sabotage of oil production facilities; and the nightmarish logistical problems that would be unavoidable in staging and sustaining operations in an area thousands of miles distant from suitable U.S. military bases. These and other factors have led at least

11. *Annual Defense Department Report FY 1976 and FY 197T*, p. III-44.

12. See, for example, Robert W. Tucker, "American Force: The Missing Link in the Oil Crisis," *Washington Post*, January 5, 1975, and Miles Ignotus [pseudonym], "Seizing Arab Oil," *Harper's Magazine*, March 1975.

one study to conclude that U.S. intervention in the Gulf is probably infeasible.[13]

THESE REGIONAL CONSIDERATIONS, in conjunction with the military, technological, and political constraints upon the amphibious mission discussed above by no means justify elimination of U.S. amphibious assault capabilities. Raids and small-scale tactical landings designed to facilitate progress of friendly forces ashore will remain militarily feasible and could play a significant role in future conflicts. However, taken together, these constraints do strongly suggest that continued Marine Corps fixation on the amphibious mission is unwarranted in light of foreseeable military requirements and growing domestic political opposition to the use of U.S. military forces in general. The principal implication of the declining viability and importance of the amphibious mission, itself one of many missions performed by the Corps during its two-hundred-year-old history, is the availability of some portion of USMC forces for alternative missions.

13. Library of Congress, Congressional Research Service, *Oil Fields as Military Objectives: A Feasibility Study*, prepared for the Special Subcommittee on Investigations of the House Committee on International Relations (GPO, 1975).

CHAPTER FIVE

TACTICAL AIR POWER: WHO WILL DO WHAT?

Closely tied to the amphibious mission's future prospects are those of Marine Corps aviation. Indeed, despite some notable incongruities between structure and role, the present peculiarities and separate status accorded Marine aviation are still justified because of their role in the no less distinctive amphibious mission. Since aviation consumes such a large—and apparently growing—percentage of funds allocated to the Corps, some of which might be spent on other programs, it warrants special attention. Can, for example, the Marine Corps justify the need for and the cost of a self-contained tactical air force?

Doctrine versus Practice

Amphibious assault against resolute defenses is the contingency for which Marine aviation—like its ground counterpart—is primarily structured. According to Marine Corps doctrine, an amphibious task force designed to support such an assault would include the amphibious assault ships themselves, a carrier task group composed of one or more carriers, each with a composite air wing,[1] and a varying number of escort and support ships.

If the element of complete tactical surprise were not considered imperative, an advance force including the carrier air groups would precede the main assault force to prepare the target area for landing by conducting reconnaissance, minesweeping, naval bombardment, and tactical air operations. During this pre-assault phase, the bulk of the aerial sorties would

1. Carrier air wings, like Marine wings, are task oriented. Typically, a wing on the newer carriers would be composed of two fighter squadrons, each equipped with twelve F-4 or F-14 aircraft; three light attack squadrons, each having twelve A-7s; one medium attack squadron consisting of twelve A-6s; and a variety of support and special mission aircraft, such as reconnaissance and electronic warfare planes.

be conducted by Navy carrier-based aircraft, assisted perhaps by some Marine planes.[2] F-14s and F-4s would be mainly responsible for attaining air superiority over the area and for defending the carrier task force against enemy attack. A-6 and A-7 aircraft, augmented where possible by land-based aircraft, would soften beach defenses.

With the arrival of the main body of the assault shipping, air defense measures would be intensified and preplanned close air strikes would be conducted against enemy installations in the landing areas and against projected helicopter landing zones. Harriers (AV-8s) aboard amphibious ships would join the carrier-based forces in ground attack operations. These suppression attacks would continue until the initial waves of Marine ground forces reached the beach, after which air support would be shifted to other targets.

Once the Marine units had established their positions on the beachhead, Marine aircraft would begin phasing ashore. Within two or three days Harriers could commence operations from beach sites, while continuing to be supported logistically from ships offshore. Construction of short airfields for tactical support would also start as soon as possible. These are rapidly constructible airstrips consisting of short aluminum runways, equipped like carriers, with catapult and arresting gear. As such SATS became available, Marine fixed-wing fighter aircraft would start moving ashore from nearby friendly land bases, or from the continental United States with the aid of in-flight refueling.[3] When the appropriate control agencies were ready to operate on the beach, the command of air operations would pass from the amphibious task force commander (a naval officer) to the landing force commander (a Marine officer) ashore; once

2. The extent to which Marine squadrons are routinely deployed aboard carriers, though undisclosed, is probably small; it is unlikely that present policy calls for more than three or four carrier-based Marine combat squadrons at any time. Moreover, though all Marine aviators are initially trained for carrier operations, only a small proportion of them are able to maintain their qualifications for these demanding operations, particularly in their night and all-weather aspects. It is worth noting that Marine squadrons, when deployed aboard carriers, become "naval aviation" squadrons. That is, in contrast to being dedicated to supporting Marine ground operations, they are there for any mission that the carrier may be called upon to perform.

3. Estimates vary on how soon SATS fields could be made operational. In congressional testimony in 1971, the Marines estimated that it would require ten to twenty days depending on the terrain. (See *Close Air Support*, Hearings before the Special Subcommittee on Close Air Support, Senate Committee on Armed Services, 92:1 [GPO, 1971], p. 263.) More recently, Marine Corps sources have indicated that SATS complexes could be installed within four or five days. (See Brooke Nihart, "U.S. Marine Corps—1975," *Air Force*, October 1975, p. 38.)

forces ashore were relatively secure, doctrine calls for carriers to depart the area, for reasons explained by Admiral Elmo Zumwalt, former chief of naval operations:

> Let's suppose that we had to land Marines to support the northern flank of NATO in Norway . . . we would have to get our carriers out of there just as soon as the Marines were ashore and had an airstrip. We did it in World War II under a far more permissive situation. We would have to do so in order to get back to the job of protecting the sea lines of communication against a tremendous threat.[4]

Many of these intricate doctrinal prescriptions are rarely followed in practice. For example, since World War II Marine aviation has operated almost exclusively from land bases and not from carriers. Moreover, in both the Korean and Vietnam conflicts the missions of Marine air units with few exceptions differed little from those of the Air Force and the Navy. Indeed, in both cases, Marine aviation was lumped together with that of the other services under the control of the single manager for air in the combat theater; the particular cut of a pilot's uniform or the service markings on his aircraft had little operational significance. This arrangement at times resulted in Navy and Marine pilots flying close air support for Army ground formations and the Air Force supporting Marine ground units. Though the distinction between Marine aviation and the air forces of the other services has become blurred over the past three decades, the Marines nonetheless cling tenaciously to their traditional role. With Vietnam behind them, they were quick to return to their heritage. According to General Cushman:

> We are re-directing our attention seaward, and re-emphasizing our partnership with the Navy and our shared concern in the Maritime aspects of our strategy.[5]

Dominant Issues

Against this background a number of issues arise that bear directly on the present course of Marine aviation. In general they stem from conflicting views regarding the specific aviation missions for which the Marines should

4. "Testimony of Admiral Elmo R. Zumwalt, Jr.," *Fiscal Year 1974 Authorization for Military Procurement, Research and Development, Construction Authorization for the Safeguard ABM, and Active Duty and Selected Reserve Strengths*, Hearings before the Senate Committee on Armed Services, 93:1 (GPO, 1973), pt. 2, p. 677.

5. Quoted by A. R. Pytko, "An Epoch of Need," *Marine Corps Gazette*, vol. 57 (May 1973), p. 48.

be responsible, the proper mix and necessary numbers of aircraft to fulfill those missions, and the appropriate doctrine governing their use.

Fighter Modernization

The selection of an aircraft to replace the aging F-4 in the Marine inventory has been a source of controversy since the early seventies. Originally, the F-14 Tomcat was chosen by the Department of the Navy to replace both the Navy and Marine Corps F-4 fleets. The F-14, the most expensive fighter yet introduced into the U.S. inventory, is a multiple-purpose aircraft. Justified primarily on the grounds that it enhances carrier survival against a sophisticated air attack, the F-14 also is seen as serving in a fighter sweep role to clear contested air space of enemy fighters and in an escort role to protect strike aircraft. Finally, it is contended that the F-14, with the basic range, performance traits, and build necessary to deliver large payloads against ground targets, could be adapted for interdiction, and perhaps even close air support missions.

The F-14 procurement program, as envisioned in April 1971, would have equipped each of the Navy's modern carriers and each Marine air wing with two squadrons of F-14s at an average unit cost of about $11.8 million. As the procurement program was cut back, estimates of unit costs mounted—reaching $17 million by July of that year—and the Marines began having second thoughts, described by General Cushman in 1973:

At the present time I prefer the F-4J [Phantom] with maneuvering slats. My predecessor in studying the problem made his study at a time when there was a price differential of only about $3 million per airplane between the F-4J and the F-14. Now that the price difference per plane may run $8 to $12 million and in my opinion, since the F-4J with the slotted wing can defeat the enemy aircraft threat against an enemy beachhead, I do not need the F-14. . . . The Marine Corps cannot afford them.[6]

The Navy thought otherwise:

I would worry about the change in doctrine that would be involved in the Navy having to continue to maintain air superiority over a beachhead with the greatly reduced number of carriers to which we have been driven, much less than in World War II. As we did in World War II, we would want to get away from the beachhead just as fast as we could in order to have the sea room and the flexibility

6. "Testimony of General Robert E. Cushman, Jr.," *Fiscal Year 1974 Authorization for Military Procurement, Research and Development, Construction Authorization for the Safeguard ABM, and Active Duty and Selected Reserve Strengths*, Hearings before the Senate Committee on Armed Services, 93:1 (GPO, 1973), pt. 2, p. 642.

of being able to deal with the threat of distances. And, therefore, I think we would find ourselves in the position of abandoning the Marines to a very great air threat under some circumstances if they did not have the F-14 ashore.[7]

Undoubtedly influencing the Navy's position was an anticipated reduction in unit cost on the order of $2 million per aircraft that would stem from a bigger, joint Navy and Marine Corps procurement program.

Not surprisingly the views of the larger, more powerful service prevailed. Within days following his testimony against Marine procurement of the F-14, the commandant abruptly changed his mind.

Over the weekend, the CNO and the Secretary of the Navy and I . . . have been hard at work. We were more or less taking the view that, because of the expense of the aircraft, because of the problems of two different programs, we had better consider perhaps the fighter force of the Navy and Marine Corps as a whole and put it together. In this way the Marine Corps could help the CNO in his concern of getting to the scene of the action and delivering the landing force. . . .

With this in mind, I told the Secretary that if I could have what I considered the proper number of aircraft, F-14s, and thus preserve the moneys that had been set aside for Marine Corps to be for Marine Corps, I thought taking an advanced fighter could well be of value to the Marine Corps. We would be getting a much better airplane.[8]

Thus the Marine Corps traded the opportunity to procure 138 F-4Js (then costing roughly $890 million) for a claim on 68 F-14As (with an estimated cost of about $1.2 billion)—enough to equip four squadrons.

Many believed the Marines were being force-fed a costly aircraft that the Corps neither needed nor wanted. Some people assigned more Machiavellian motives to the Navy. As early as May 1975, one commentator observed that "the Marines, going back to long experience in which the Navy has managed to corner the hottest airplanes while saddling Marine squadrons with older, less desirable models, feel that . . . so-called Marine F-14s will later, if not sooner, end up on Navy flight decks while Marines get lower quality F-18s in return."[9]

He was right. In August 1975, General Louis H. Wilson, the new commandant, announced that the twelve Marine Corps fighter squadrons would remain an all F-4 force, to be replaced by F-18s in the early 1980s. The F-14s previously earmarked for the Corps would be diverted to the

7. "Testimony of Admiral Elmo R. Zumwalt, Jr.," ibid., p. 677.

8. Testimony of Robert E. Cushman, Jr., *Department of Defense Appropriations for 1974*, Hearings before a Subcommittee of the House Committee on Appropriations, 93:1 (GPO, 1973), pt. 2, p. 394.

9. R. D. Heinl, Jr., "Marine Corps in Middle on Fighter Plane Choice," *Detroit News*, May 22, 1975.

Navy thus providing the Navy with eighteen instead of fourteen F-14 squadrons. In his announcement, General Wilson said:

We are reaffirming a basic concept that air defenses in the initial stages of an amphibious operation will be provided by carrier based Navy aircraft. We are also giving full consideration to the fact that once the Marines are ashore, we are normally operating in an austere support environment.[10]

Whether or not the Marines eventually will be equipped with the twin-engine F-18, however, remains uncertain. Shortly after the aircraft was selected, critics charged that the Navy was flouting a congressional mandate. In order to keep costs down, the Congress in 1974 had indicated that the new Navy fighter should be a derivative of the F-16, the Air Force's new combat fighter.[11] Moreover, reports that the cost of the F-18 program would exceed earlier estimates by as much as $1.8 billion apparently caused concern among administration officials. Office of Management and Budget analysts are reported to have asked: "Is there a lower cost alternative to the F-18?"[12]

The answer depends in part on whether it is considered necessary for Marine aircraft to be capable of operating aboard carriers. Marine aircraft have not been deployed aboard U.S. carriers in significant numbers since World War II, and, with the decline in the number of available carriers, it is unlikely that Marine aviators will see much carrier duty in the future. Because stiff financial and performance penalties accompany aircraft designed for carrier operations, the key to a lower-cost fighter would appear to lie in the willingness to sever the Corps' link to carrier operations. In that case, the simpler F-16, costing about $3 million per aircraft less than the F-18—or the even lower-cost F-5—could meet any threat that the Marines are likely to face and at the same time should be easier than the F-18 to maintain in the austere environments envisioned for Marine operations.

Both the Navy and the Marine Corps, however, can be expected to oppose strongly any move to denude the Marine Corps of carrier-capable aircraft. For the Navy's part, Marine Corps squadrons represent a pool of "naval" aircraft that could be used to offset combat attrition that might

10. Department of Defense, News Release, August 1, 1975.

11. *Making Appropriations for the Department of Defense, Fiscal Year 1975*, H. Rept. 93-1363, 93:2 (GPO, 1974), p. 27. Subsequently, however, the General Accounting Office, which had been petitioned by an aerospace contractor to void the F-18 choice, agreed with the Navy that the selection "complied with the letter and the spirit of the Fiscal 1975 Defense Appropriation Act." (See "GAO Upholds Navy in Choice of F-18," *Aviation Week*, October 6, 1975, p. 19.)

12. "OMB Questions F-18 Cost Effectiveness," *Aviation Week*, June 23, 1975, p. 18.

accompany future conflict. Additionally, the lower unit cost associated with common Navy and Marine Corps procurement is attractive to Navy officials charged with selling aircraft programs to Congress.[13]

On the other hand, the Marines are fearful of the potential implications of being equipped with aircraft indistinguishable from Air Force fighters. They would want to avoid the obvious question that would follow: should the Marine Corps have an independent fighter and attack role at all?

The Air Superiority–Deep Interdiction Issue

As indicated above, a substantial share of Marine resources is devoted to procuring and operating aircraft designed mainly for air superiority and interdiction missions. Could the Marine Corps eliminate this costly role and, instead, rely on the Navy and the Air Force, which are already structured and doctrinally oriented to undertake such missions?

MARINE EMPHASIS ON CLOSE AIR SUPPORT. Without these missions Marine tactical aviation would be limited to close air support, which the Marine Corps not only pioneered but to which it is more fully dedicated than the other services. Such a restructuring, however, would represent a radical departure from the concept of the integrated Marine air and ground team, which has been considered vital to combined operations—particularly amphibious assaults. Those against this departure from doctrine presume that the only source of sustained air support would be Marine air units staging from SATS complexes. Marine ground operations, so their argument goes, are likely to be conducted outside of the range of land-based Air Force fighter aircraft and Navy carriers, which, according to prescribed doctrine, would leave as soon as the Marines had secured the beach.

It is not at all clear, however, that for the contingencies in which the Marines are most likely to become involved, air superiority and interdiction support would be necessary in the first place. Such operations would be of marginal importance in Asia where most potential adversaries neither pose a threat to U.S. air supremacy nor possess a logistic infrastructure against which an interdiction campaign would be profitable. Moreover, where those air missions are considered necessary to the success of Marine ground

13. For example, if the Marines were not included in the proposed F-18 program, the total number of aircraft to be bought would be reduced from 811 to about 560. The smaller quantity would increase the average program unit cost from $9.6 million to about $11.3 million per airplane. (Data derived from "F-18 Congressional Data Sheet," *Aerospace Daily*, June 2, 1975, reverse of p. 173.)

operations, it is unlikely that situations would arise in which the Marines would find themselves bereft of both Air Force and Navy air support. Sustained operations by Marine forces in, say, North Korea, would certainly be a part of a combined campaign for which Air Force support would be readily available from land bases in South Korea. Land-based Air Force aircraft could also be expected to support Marine operations in the Mediterranean along the southern flank of NATO. On the other hand, along the northern NATO flank (for example, Norway), along the eastern littorals of the Mediterranean, or in the Persian Gulf, the Marines could count less on Air Force support. Gaining initial air superiority in these regions would most probably be left to Navy carrier-based aircraft. The areas are outside the range of Air Force or Marine land-based aircraft, unless they are refueled in flight. As existing airfields became available or were occupied, however, Air Force strike aircraft could take over.

According to stated doctrine, once the Marines have established a foothold ashore, the Navy wants to get its carriers out to sea where they are less vulnerable and where they have other work to do. Whether carriers could remain in the target area, in fact, depends on their chances of survival and on the importance of their sea control mission.

CARRIER SURVIVABILITY. The survivability of aircraft carriers, itself an issue of widespread and often heated controversy, is too complex to be dealt with in detail in this study. In brief, carrier critics point to the threat to U.S. carrier forces in the European theater posed by Soviet land-based aircraft (particularly bombers equipped with air-to-surface guided missiles), nuclear-powered attack submarines, and cruise missiles. They question whether carriers would be able to remain on station without undue risk in areas where the Soviet Union could concentrate land-based aircraft or submarines against them.[14] If this assessment is correct, then amphibious assaults along either flank of NATO would be infeasible. Carrier protagonists, on the other hand, argue that carriers, if permitted freedom of movement, are not so vulnerable with their great mobility and panoply of defensive weapons and that projection of both air and land combat power ashore on the European littorals is a critical and feasible mission. The Navy has structured its forces accordingly. If this judgment is correct, the question left hanging is the extent to which the threat to the carrier's ability to survive is aggravated if it has to remain on station after Marine aircraft

14. For a discussion of the usefulness of carriers in a NATO scenario, see Charles L. Schultze and others, *Setting National Priorities: The 1972 Budget* (Brookings Institution, 1971), pp. 71–81.

operations have been established ashore—beyond a period of from five to twenty days. Survivability probably would be resolved within the first few days of a war between NATO and the Warsaw Pact, most assuredly within the first three weeks. Moreover, if it is argued that carriers should leave the target area to survive, then so too should the amphibious task force, which would become even more vulnerable once the carriers have left.

For contingencies less demanding than a NATO war, the case for carrier withdrawal is even less compelling. In conflicts not involving the USSR, particularly in Asia, survivability is not a vital concern. Against threats that could be met by amphibious assault operations in the Pacific, the supporting carrier task forces could be expected to remain on station with virtual impunity, as they did in the Tonkin Gulf during U.S. participation in the Vietnam War.

SEA CONTROL. Another argument put forth for early departure of carriers from the target area is that they would be needed to protect shipping lanes worldwide. Some military analysts contend that a war in Europe against the Soviet Union would soon spill over into Asia, thus requiring protection of U.S. sea lines of communication in the Pacific. Such a replay of World War II, however, is difficult for many to envision because it assumes that a conventional war with the Soviets could reach global proportions before escalating into nuclear conflict.

In truth, the sea control mission is important mainly in the event of a protracted war in Europe. Carriers, in conjunction with land-based antisubmarine aircraft, would be used to counter the formidable Soviet submarine threat. Thus it is argued that carriers could be available for only a limited period to support amphibious assault forces, particularly on the northern flank of Europe, in which case Marine fighters operating from SATS complexes would be the only source of continuous air support to Marine forces.

There are two important and related counterarguments to this reasoning.

First, many analysts maintain that a war in Europe would not last long enough for a full Marine division to be employed on the northern flank of NATO. According to this view, a conventional war in Europe would end, either in negotiation or in escalation to nuclear conflict, long before a Marine division would be capable of mounting a division-sized amphibious assault—an estimated forty-five to sixty days after a decision to mount such an assault was made.

Second, even if a European war were protracted and Marines were used on the northern flank, say, to reinforce Norway, the requirement for air support would hinge in large part on whether the landing was opposed. As pointed out in chapter 4, an amphibious assault against the Soviet-occupied Norwegian beaches would be unduly risky and of dubious value; thus it is highly probable that a Marine amphibious operation on the northern flank would be successful only if uncontested.

In short, the contention that the Marines, if obliged to count on the Air Force and the Navy for air superiority and deep interdiction support, would find themselves unprotected does not appear well founded. In the most plausible contingencies for which the Marines would need counterair or interdiction support, it could be provided by the Air Force and Navy.

EFFECT ON THE SIZE OF THE MARINE CORPS. Relieving the Marine Corps of the counterair and interdiction missions would entail phasing out the F-4 and A-6 squadrons. Although F-4s have been used for close support, there is little question that they are designed mainly for air superiority and interdiction. How A-6 squadrons would be employed, on the other hand, is unclear. Though Marine aviation doctrine lists close air support as the principal mission for the A-6, the aircraft's performance characteristics and avionics package suggest capabilities as well or perhaps better suited to the interdiction role.

Even if the close air support mission is considered paramount, however, the case can still be made for removing A-6s from the Marine inventory, albeit on somewhat different grounds. In contrast to A-4 and AV-8 aircraft, which are used mainly in visual daylight operations demanding the intimate coordination embodied in the integrated ground and air team concept, A-6s are designed principally for night and all-weather operations, which are essentially automatic. When employed for this purpose, the A-6 uses a radar offset bombing system, which targets on a ground radar beacon positioned by a forward air controller assigned to the Marine ground formation. For this type of operation, the argument for a close working harmony between air and ground components is less persuasive. It would appear that Navy carrier-based A-6 squadrons, which are trained to perform similar maneuvers, could be counted upon to provide close air sorties under adverse weather conditions. Moreover, the relatively sophisticated A-6E system may be inappropriate for the austere support environment envisioned for Marine aviation operations.

The financial savings from this change would hinge on national requirements for air superiority and deep interdiction capabilities. If the total number of such squadrons now currently planned is deemed critical to

U.S. national security, dollar savings would be small, perhaps nonexistent.[15] Alternatively, the assumption that the Air Force and Navy could provide air superiority and deep interdiction support for the Marine Corps within their presently programmed resources would call for reducing by seventeen the total number of U.S. fighter and attack squadrons. Those who hold this view point to the difficulty of evaluating the contribution made by seventeen Marine squadrons out of a total of 114 squadrons now in the U.S. inventory capable of performing such missions.[16] Moreover, the Air Force and the Navy are in the process of substantially increasing their fighter forces. Plans to increase Air Force tactical wings from twenty-two to twenty-six have recently been divulged. The bulk of this increase will result from the procurement of a mix of sophisticated F-15 fighters and simpler F-16 lightweight fighters over the next five years. The Navy, meanwhile, has selected the F-18 as its lightweight fighter and hopes eventually to procure about 300 of these aircraft for the fighter role. These changes, taken together, suggest a future Air Force and Navy fighter posture of sufficient size to support any type of foreseeable contingency, including those in which the Marines would be involved.

Disbanding seventeen Marine F-4 and A-6 squadrons would result in average savings in operating and support costs of about $680 million a year

15. Many would argue that the transfer of the fighter and attack missions to the Navy and Air Force would cost more because the Marines can operate the aircraft at a lower cost. Such an analysis, however, is made difficult by the accounting problems discussed in chapter 3.

16. The appropriate number of tactical aircraft needed is a most difficult conceptual problem on which defense analysts differ sharply. The usual approach to the design of military forces involves "force matching"—examining the manpower and equipment comparisons of friendly and enemy forces under a given set of assumptions. For tactical air capabilities, the task is made all the more difficult by the diversity of missions that can be performed by each aircraft and the sensitivity of aircraft levels to assumptions about sortie rates, attrition, duration of combat, differences in the quality of pilots, ordnance and logistic support, and so forth. Further complicating the analysis are the differing perceptions within the Pentagon of the contribution made by Marine tactical aviation. The commandant, viewing the amphibious role as preeminent, deems the integrated ground and air team as critical to the conduct of amphibious operations. The secretary of the navy, on the other hand, regards Marine and Navy air assets as a collective capability useful for prosecuting, in addition to amphibious operations, the other missions for which the Navy is responsible: sea control, projection of air power ashore, and naval presence. Finally, the secretary of defense considers Marine aviation to be a part of a pool of total national tactical aviation resources to be employed in whatever roles are necessary to meet any contingency. It is worth noting, however, that in both the Korean and Vietnam Wars the Marines vigorously opposed the use of their aviation for missions other than those to support their own ground units.

over the next decade and in reduced aircraft procurement amounting to some $2 billion.

Apart from the financial implications, removing the air superiority and interdiction missions from the Marine Corps could have consequences for the overall quality of Marine manpower in ground combat units. Because personnel assigned to aviation units require a higher level of technical aptitude and intelligence, a larger proportion of high school graduates are assigned to aviation units.[17] It is reasonable to expect that a larger number of these individuals would be available to ground units if aviation billets were reduced.

Consolidating Close Air Support

The likelihood that future conflict will find the Marine Corps fighting, as it often has in the past, alongside the Army indicates less need for a separate Marine air capability as epitomized in the air and ground team concept. Under certain conditions, consolidating tactical air operations in a single service has important advantages; sorties could be allocated more efficiently, and redundant logistical support requirements could be eliminated.

This issue is not new. Many have questioned the proliferation of separate tactical air forces; according to one of the most vocal congressional critics, Senator Barry Goldwater:

> We had hearings . . . around 1950. We set out the roles and missions of tactical air; and since that time instead of having one tactical air force we now have four. It is to this point that I think the Defense Department is showing weakness in not being willing to face up to the growing fact that we are finding it increasingly difficult . . . to support the tremendous cost involved . . .[18]

The rationale for the separate tactical air capabilities is elusive. Who should provide close air support to whom has been an unresolved and controversial question among the services since the initial Key West Agreement of 1948, a specific statement of the roles and missions of the four services that were broadly defined in the National Security Act of 1947. The most recent comprehensive study of tactical air power, made public by the Department of Defense in 1971, concentrated on a related issue: the

17. At last count, three-fourths of those assigned to aviation units had completed high school, compared with 54 percent in ground units. (See *Fiscal Year 1976 and July–September 1976 Transition Period Authorization for Military Procurement, Research and Development, and Active Duty, Selected Reserve and Civilian Personnel Strengths*, Hearing before the Senate Committee on Armed Services, 94:1 [GPO, 1975], pt. 3, p. 1415.)

18. *Close Air Support*, Hearings, p. 58.

need for simultaneous development of three aircraft for close air support—the Air Force's A-X (now called the A-10), the Army's Cheyenne, and the Marine Corps' Harrier. Although the study group did *not* meet the separate service issue head on, its conclusion that all three aircraft "offer sufficiently different capabilities for our future forces to justify continuing all three programs at the present time" endorsed implicitly the maintenance of three separate close air support forces.[19]

That both national security and institutional interests have played a part in the evolution of current tactical air structure and the services' roles and missions is generally agreed. There is less consensus on the degree of influence that each has exerted. The current Marine Corps position, however, is quite clear, and succinctly stated by its former deputy chief of staff for air and the former commanding general of the Third Marine Amphibious Force in Vietnam:

The Marine Corps is proud of the fact that it is a force of combined arms, and it jealously guards the integrity of its air-ground team. Retention of operational control of its air arm is important to the Corps' air-ground team, as air constitutes a significant part of its offensive fire power. Ever since the Korean War, when the 1st Marine Division was under the operational control of the Eighth Army and the 1st MAW was under the Fifth Air Force, the Corps has been especially alert to avoid such a split again.[20]

Such views go far beyond institutional self-preservation. The Marines hold strong convictions, shared by many non-Marines, that every Marine is *first* a rifleman. This credo, it is argued, ensures that Marine pilots make an extra effort to support their fellow Marines on the ground—men with whom they fight, train, and socialize. Also apparently in the minds of many Marines is the low priority accorded the close air support mission by the Air Force and Navy, upon which the Marines would have to rely in the absence of organic air power. The U.S. Air Force has traditionally assigned highest priority to air superiority and deep interdiction missions, whereas the Navy has put most of its emphasis on fleet defense.[21]

19. Ibid., p. 410.

20. Keith B. McCutcheon, "Marine Aviation in Vietnam, 1962–1970," in U.S. Naval Institute, *Proceedings*, May 1971, pp. 134–35.

21. Under external pressures, the Air Force appears to be shifting rapidly toward greater emphasis on close air support, however; witness the relatively large program to procure A-10 aircraft geared to that mission. To the extent that this represents a legitimate reordering of Air Force mission priorities, less forceful are the arguments for a separate Marine close air support capability. Those who anticipate that the Air Force at first opportunity will unload A-10s on the reserves, as it did A-37s, are taking a wait-and-see attitude.

Advocates of consolidated air operations point to World War II experience. In the early days of the Allied campaign in North Africa, for example, the practice of assigning air units to specific Army ground units—much like the current Marine division-wing concept—gave way to the establishment of expanded tactical air commands to counter centralized German tactics. The organic aviation concept, it is estimated, with each division having its own air units, would have called for 9,000 U.S. fighter aircraft to support the seventy-five U.S. divisions in Europe and the Mediterranean during World War II, whereas the actual number of U.S. fighters committed against Germany in 1945 was about 6,000. Today, such an organic distribution of aviation assets would require that *all* U.S. Air Force fighter aircraft be committed to the close air support of Army units at the expense of other missions.[22]

Over the strong objections of the Marine Corps, proponents of the single management concept prevailed in both the Vietnam and Korean Wars. Precipitated mainly by the battle for Khe Sanh in 1968, all U.S. aviation assets in Southeast Asia were placed under the "management" of a single commander for air (an Air Force general officer). This arrangement found Marine aircraft flying some close air sorties in support of Army forces and Air Force aircraft sometimes supporting the Marines.

Though obviously unhappy, the Marine air commander concluded in retrospect:

> The system worked. Both the Air Force and the Marines saw to that. But the way it was made to work evolved over a period of time, and a lot of it was due to gentlemen's agreements between on-the-scene commanders.[23]

Thus experience since the end of World War II strongly suggests that the Marines' air and ground team doctrine, a prerequisite for assault amphibious operations, is less relevant when the Marines are engaged in sustained inland combat campaigns. The advantages of relieving the Marine Corps of the close air support mission parallels those of the air superiority and interdiction missions. Again, financial implications would depend on an assessment of what the Air Force and Navy could do with their existing capabilities. Transferring actual resources along with the close air support mission would yield little savings. The principal benefit in that case would be measured in terms of the reduction in aviation manpower billets and the possibility of improving the quality of Marine ground forces. On the other hand, phasing out Marine aviation units without offsetting increases—

22. See "Testimony of General Momyer," *Close Air Support*, Hearings, p. 189.
23. Keith B. McCutcheon, "Marine Aviation in Vietnam, 1962–1970," p. 137.

based on the judgment that close air support resources now programmed for the Air Force and Navy are sufficient—would result in substantial dollar savings.

WHAT IS THE FUTURE role of Marine aviation? The Marine Corps now spends 55 percent or more of its limited resources on an independent air arm. The issues are: (1) should the Corps be in the air superiority and interdiction business? (2) how should the Marines modernize their fleet of F-4 aircraft? and (3) should the Marine Corps even have its own close air support capability?

We conclude that the Marines should eliminate their air superiority and interdiction missions and phase out their squadrons of F-4 and A-6 aircraft. If such a measure is judged inappropriate, modernization of the F-4 fleet should be restricted to a simple lightweight fighter design less costly to procure and operate than either the F-14 or F-18. And, for any Marine ground forces that may be reoriented from amphibious to nonamphibious operations, an organic close air support capability need not be provided.

CHAPTER SIX

RECRUITMENT: CAN ENOUGH "GOOD" MEN BE FOUND?

Whatever the future tasks of Marine Corps ground and tactical aviation, the Corps' ability to carry them out effectively will depend to no small degree upon its capacity to attract and mold a sufficient number of qualified men. No investigation of alternative postures for the USMC can ignore the potential implications for Marine recruitment of the all-volunteer environment. When military conscription ended in 1973, the armed forces faced, for the first time since 1948, the challenge of obtaining their manpower solely by voluntary means. Between 1948 and 1973 the draft was used mainly to man the Army; however, by inducing those not interested in serving in the Army to enlist in the Navy, Marine Corps, and Air Force it indirectly filled their ranks as well. Yet among all the services the Marine Corps relied least on these so-called draft-motivated volunteers. This stemmed in part from its relatively small size and the small number of new recruits required each year, and in part from its attraction for at least one particular segment of American youth.[1]

As shown in table 6-1, the Marines' ability to attract a higher proportion of "true" volunteers—those who would have been expected to enlist despite, not because of, the draft—exceeded that of any other service even before the transition to the all-volunteer armed forces got under way.

This encouraging record suggested that the Marines would encounter

1. Surveys conducted between 1971 and 1973 indicated that among male civilians between the ages of sixteen and twenty-one who wanted to enlist in the military services, about 10 percent indicated that the Marine Corps would be their first choice. In this group, the two positive characteristics for which the Marine Corps rated highest among the services were "proving manhood" and "attractive uniform"; it ranked third among the services for "exciting life." In all other characteristics listed—"pay," "family living conditions," "chance to get ahead," "learn useful skills," "use skills and abilities," and "foreign travel"—the Marines ranked lowest. (See Department of Defense, Manpower Research and Data Analysis Center, "Attitudes of Youth toward Military Service in the All-Volunteer Force" [1974; processed], p. 42.)

Table 6-1. Enlistment of Male True Volunteers, by Service, Fiscal Years 1971–73[a]
True volunteers in thousands

	1971		*1972*		*1973*	
Service	*True volunteers*	*Percentage of total enlistments*	*True volunteers*	*Percentage of total enlistments*	*True volunteers*	*Percentage of total enlistments*
Marine Corps	39	71	45	84	49	94
Navy	43	57	67	79	80	84
Army	85	58	110	73	151	83
Air Force	48	53	58	72	76	85

Source: "The All-Volunteer Force and the End of the Draft," Special Report of the Secretary of Defense Elliott L. Richardson (March 1973; processed), pp. 5–8.

a. True volunteers are those who freely chose to enter the military forces despite the draft. For a description of the procedures that were used by the Department of Defense to measure true volunteers, see Martin Binkin and John D. Johnston, *All-Volunteer Armed Forces: Progress, Problems, and Prospects*, Report prepared for the Senate Committee on Armed Services, 93:1 (GPO, 1973), pp. 8, 9.

few difficulties in meeting their quantitative requirements for manpower. Indeed, the Marines chose not to fall into step with the other services, which in varying degrees sought to attract sufficient volunteers by increasing monetary incentives, providing better living conditions, relaxing grooming and disciplinary standards, and by widely advertising that they were in tune with the new youth culture. In contrast to the Army recruiting slogan "Today's Army Wants to Join You" and the Navy's "Sailors Have More Fun," the Corps' theme of "The Marines Are Looking for a Few Good Men" reflects the elitist attitude that they have maintained in the all-volunteer environment.

Progress

Anticipation that the Marines could recruit sufficient numbers of men proved well founded, notwithstanding the small end-strength deficit of about 7,000 in fiscal 1974. In terms of quality and representation, however, results have been mixed.

Quality

Quality has not been easy to define. Job performance depends on a variety of factors. Included are such characteristics as mental ability, level of education, job aptitude, experience, motivation, loyalty, diligence, adaptability, and ability to get along with coworkers. All are interrelated and their

Table 6-2. Percentage Distribution of Marine Recruits by AFQT Mental Group, Fiscal Years 1971–75

Mental category	*1971*	*1972*	*1973*	*1974*	*1975*
I and II (above average)	26	25	25	33	36
III (average)	55	55	61	60	60
IV (below average)	19	20	15	8	4
Average score	49.0	48.1	50.8	56.7	n.a.

Source: Data provided by United States Marine Corps, Headquarters, September 1975.
n.a. Not available.

relative importance varies by type of job, as well as by experience level within a given occupation. The two yardsticks most frequently used by the armed forces to measure quality are standardized test scores and level of education. The former are closely related to performance in a training environment; the latter is generally accepted as a better basis for predicting behavior.

In terms of standardized test scores,[2] the quality of recruits, according to Marine Corps data, has improved markedly since the end of the draft (table 6-2). These reports indicate a substantial increase in volunteers with above average scores, a modest increase in volunteers with average scores, and a dramatic decrease in enlistees with below average scores. In fact, in fiscal 1975 the Marine Corps ranked second only to the Air Force in recruiting fewer volunteers who scored in the below average category.

In terms of another measure—level of education attained—the Ma-

2. Standardized tests are administered to all new personnel. The most commonly used standard is the mental group designation based on scores of the Armed Forces Qualification Test (AFQT). This test encompasses word knowledge, arithmetic reasoning, tool knowledge, and pattern analysis. On the basis of test scores, examinees are divided into the following groups ranging from very high military aptitude (Category I) to very low military aptitude (Category V):

Mental category	*Percentile score*
I	93 to 100
II	65 to 92
III	31 to 64
IV	10 to 30
V	9 and below

The AFQT is used principally to differentiate between Mental Groups I and II (above average), III (average), and IV and V (below average). Test scores below 10 (Mental Group V) disqualify an individual from military service by law. Those scoring below the thirtieth percentile (Mental Group IV) are considered by the services to require more training and generally present greater disciplinary problems than those in the higher groups. The method of administering and preparing recruits to take these tests varies among the services.

Table 6-3. Percentage of High School Graduates among Recruits, by Service, Fiscal Years 1970–75

Service	*1970*	*1971*	*1972*	*1973*	*1974*	*1975*
Marine Corps	56	51	53	51	53	59
Army	70	66	71	65	56	66
Navy	76	78	76	69	70	75
Air Force	93	87	83	88	92	91

Source: Data provided by Department of Defense, July 1975.

rines have not fared as well. With the end of the draft, the Marine Corps, which traditionally lagged behind the other services in this regard, experienced a small decrease in volunteers who had completed high school. Although evidence suggested that those who had completed high school were more successful in coming to terms with military rules and regulations, the Marines made a conscious decision to concentrate on test results rather than on level of education, for reasons explained to Congress by Lieutenant General Samuel Jaskilka, deputy chief of staff for manpower:

The Marine Corps has always been concerned about quality standards in recruiting. In April 1973, we set a limit of 10% on the number to be enlisted in Mental Group IV. We established this requirement because we believe Mental Group is a reasonable predictor of trainability. This was a difficult decision because high school graduation is an indicator of "stick-to-itiveness" and that, too, is important. We desired both trainability and "stick-to-itiveness" but the recruiting market forced us to select one.[3]

On another occasion, General Jaskilka was more specific:

We have found that many who complete high school are social graduates and do not have the mental capability to be trained in Marine Corps skills. We would prefer to acquire recruits who have both amenability to discipline and the ability to absorb training but, until we have determined and allocated the optimal mix of resources to attain both, we prefer to require that the young men we recruit be trainable.[4]

The reduction in the proportion of recruits who were high school graduates that began in fiscal 1971 and that persisted for the next two years (see table 6-3) prompted Congress to require by law that in fiscal 1974 at least 55 percent of the recruits in each service be high school graduates.[5] By Depart-

3. *Fiscal Year 1975 Authorization for Military Procurement, Research and Development, and Active Duty, Selected Reserve and Civilian Personnel Strengths*, Hearings before the Senate Committee on Armed Services, 93:2 (GPO, 1974), pt. 4, p. 1395.

4. *Department of Defense Appropriations for 1975*, Hearings before a Subcommittee of the House Committee on Appropriations, 93:2 (GPO, 1974), pt. 3, p. 18.

5. *Department of Defense Appropriation Bill, 1974*, House of Representatives, 93:1 (GPO, 1973), p. 19.

ment of Defense estimate, the Marines came very close to meeting that requirement in fiscal 1974—they recruited about 53 percent—but only by sacrificing quantity; they ended the year some 7,000 personnel, or 3.6 percent, short of their total strength goal of about 196,000. A redirection of recruiting efforts and a revision of recruitment standards appears to have paid off in fiscal 1975. The Marines finished the year strong; by their estimates, 59 percent of the men and women entering in fiscal 1975 had completed high school.

Racial Composition

The steady growth in the proportion of blacks among recruits concerns those who feel that the military establishment is becoming less and less representative of the total population. Admittedly, the racial makeup of the Marine Corps has undergone significant change. The percentage of black recruits grew from about 13 percent in 1970 to 19 percent in 1975, whereas the overall percentage of blacks in the Marine Corps enlisted force increased from 11 percent to 18 percent over the same period.[6]

According to General Jaskilka, this trend presents "an adjustment problem for members of both races, most of whom have never lived in an environment with so many members of another race."[7] The fact that the heaviest concentration of blacks is found in Marine infantry units exacerbates the problem. Many rifle companies consist of from 30 to 45 percent black personnel; the Second Marine Division is close to 30 percent black. The Corps, recognizing the difficulties posed by this imbalance, is attempting to deal with it by fostering better leadership training and human relations programs, such as providing courses in race relations for top noncommissioned officers.

Disciplinary Trends

In spite of improvements in the mental ability of Marine recruits and the rising proportion of those enlisting with high school education, the Corps is

6. By comparison, blacks constitute about 13 percent of the U.S. male population aged from seventeen to twenty and about 11 percent of those aged seventeen to forty-four. (U.S. Bureau of the Census, *Census of Population, 1970: General Population Characteristics*, Final Report PC(1)-B1, *United States Summary* [1972], table 52, pp. 1-269, 1-275.)

7. Samuel Jaskilka, "Quality and Leadership." *Marine Corps Gazette*, vol. 59 (January 1975), p. 17.

Table 6-4. Trends in Disciplinary Incidents in the Military Services, Fiscal Years 1971–75
Incidents per thousand average monthly enlisted strength

Type of disciplinary incident	*1971*	*1972*	*1973*	*1974*	*1975*
Courts-martial[a]					
Marine Corps	69.5	69.5	68.6	71.6	68.9
Army	39.6	33.5	29.2	29.9	21.8
Navy	23.2	16.4	17.1	19.1	19.2
Air Force	2.8	3.3	3.5	4.0	3.4
Nonjudicial punishment[b]					
Marine Corps	266.5	280.3	328.4	412.8	367.2
Army	253.5	266.9	265.7	260.0	242.0
Navy	114.5	114.8	158.9	234.0	225.2
Air Force	34.7	48.1	51.1	56.1	58.5
Absentee incidents[c]					
Marine Corps	166.6	170.0	234.3	287.5	300.9
Army	176.9	166.4	159.0	130.0	95.4
Navy	19.0	18.3	21.7	53.8	73.0
Air Force	9.4	17.2	16.1	17.3	13.0
Desertions[d]					
Marine Corps	56.2	65.3	63.2	89.2	105.0
Army	73.5	62.0	52.0	41.2	26.8
Navy	11.1	8.8	13.6	21.2	22.4
Air Force	1.5	2.8	2.2	2.4	1.9

Source: Based on data provided by Department of Defense, Office of the Assistant Secretary for Manpower and Reserve Affairs, November 1975.

a. Courts-martial include general, special, and summary.

b. Nonjudicial punishment is meted out for violations of the Uniform Code of Military Justice that do not warrant court-martial action. Punishment is normally confined to formal written reprimand or extra duties.

c. Absentee incidents involve those who are absent without leave (AWOL) for a period of less than thirty days.

d. Those who have been AWOL for thirty or more consecutive days are administratively classified as deserters. Only after the accused is convicted of the charge of desertion can the term "deserter" be applied in the strict legal sense.

apparently beset by disciplinary problems that might affect the readiness of Marine units.

Several measures of disciplinary trends are shown in table 6-4. The striking result is that by any measure the Marine Corps is experiencing not only a significantly higher rate of disciplinary problems than any other service but also a rate that, with few exceptions, has been growing over the past several years.[8] Indeed, the desertion rate in the Marine Corps for fiscal 1975 was over ten times the rate during World War II, three times the maximum in the Korean War, over twice what it was during the height of the Vietnam

8. The services differ in their punishment and disciplinary policies; emphasis should not be placed on service comparisons. The data shown could, in part, reflect that the Marines run a tighter ship than the other services; for example, they could have stricter criteria for courts-martial.

War, and about seven times the rate prevailing in the peacetime years of the early sixties. The Corps' 1975 rates of courts-martial, absent without leave (AWOL), and desertion incidents far exceeded the combined rates of the Army, Navy, and Air Force.

Why this has occurred, if known within the Corps, has not been publicly disclosed. Many possibilities have been discussed. Some point to the turbulence created by the stringent rotational requirements associated with maintaining the large garrison in Okinawa, where Marines serve one-year tours unaccompanied by their dependents. Some place the blame on problems associated with maintaining thousands of Marines deployed continuously afloat. Others feel that the Marines are paying a price for their adherence to traditional standards and policies. And there are also critics who believe that changing racial balance lies at the root of the problem.

Finally, questions about the reliability of some qualitative recruiting statistics have been raised within the Corps. According to one concerned Marine officer:

> We could solve about 90 percent of this problem [too many marginal and substandard Marines] by tightening up our recruiting program. . . . We must stop widespread cheating on entrance tests, deliberate concealment of police records . . . and misrepresentation of birth dates.[9]

One study indicates that the Corps' relatively small proportion of high school graduates may be of significance. Of all males who entered the Marine Corps in 1972, 19.0 percent of those who had not completed high school had deserted by April 1974, compared to 5.5 percent of those who had a high school diploma. In terms of mental category, the rate of desertion was inversely proportional to the score attained on standardized tests, ranging from a desertion rate of 5.6 percent among those scoring above average, 10.8 to 13.8 percent among those in the average group, and 17.1 percent among those scoring below average. Virtually no difference was detected between racial groups; 12.3 percent of all whites and 12.9 percent of all blacks deserted. The study concludes that educational level, in combination with any or all of the other factors studied (mental group, race, age, and term of service) was the best discriminator between deserters and nondeserters.[10]

The influence of these disciplinary trends on the effectiveness of the Marine Corps is difficult to assess. That significant problems do exist, however,

9. John F. Flynn, "Finding Good Marines," *Marine Corps Gazette*, vol. 59 (June 1975), p. 42.

10. Based on data in U.S. Marine Corps, "FY 74 Deserter Profile" (USMC, Headquarters, March 1975; processed).

has been suggested by several Marine officers writing in unofficial publications. One estimated that "the three Divisions would be hard-pressed to field one full-strength division prepared for combat."[11] According to another: "My recent experience in Okinawa convinced me without a doubt that the Battalion Landing Teams that go afloat are not adequately prepared for combat or amphibious assault."[12]

And concern has not been limited to the rank and file. Shortly after assuming command of the Corps, General Louis H. Wilson expressed his strong dissatisfaction with the "deplorable" disciplinary statistics.[13] To eliminate those who are unwilling to adapt to the discipline and requirements of military life, General Wilson announced a new criterion for the Marine Corps: by fiscal 1977, 75 percent of new recruits will have high school diplomas. During the first three months of General Wilson's command, that goal was actually exceeded. Of those entering the Marine Corps in July, August, and September of 1975, 76 percent had completed their high school education. Moreover, during the same period, more than 2,000 Marines who were not considered to be amenable to the Corps' standards of discipline were discharged.[14] It is still too early to determine how these changes will influence the disciplinary problems besetting the Corps.

Prospects

Can the Corps sustain a force of 200,000 men solely by voluntary means? Answers vary, depending on different interpretations of what constitutes "acceptable" quality and "acceptable" representation and on different projections of political, social, and especially economic patterns.

Quality and representation aside, it is likely that the Marine Corps will be able to meet quantitative requirements for the indefinite future. To do so will require that about 45,000 males, or one out of every twenty-five "qualified and available" men, eventually volunteer for the Marine Corps.[15]

11. David E. Kelly, "Must the Marine Corps Shrink or Die?" *Armed Forces Journal*, October 1974, p. 18.

12. Arthur S. Weber, Jr., "Leadership and Quality," *Marine Corps Gazette*, vol. 59 (June 1975), p. 41.

13. Reported in *Washington Star*, July 14, 1975.

14. "A Conversation with the Commandant," Interview with General Wilson, *Seapower*, November 1975, p. 16.

15. The average annual demand for male enlisted volunteers is based on total enlisted requirements of 178,000 and an annual turnover of 26 percent, which in turn is based on a career/first-term ratio of 26:74 and an average duration of first-term enlistment of 2.87 years. The available pool of qualified manpower excludes those who *cannot* volunteer

Two counterbalancing factors will hold the future recruiting task rather constant. First, the supply of qualified and available manpower will decrease over the next decade as the eighteen-year-old cohort becomes smaller. At the same time, however, the long-term requirements for new recruits will tend to diminish as longer initial terms of service are instituted.[16]

One of the least certain—and most important—elements that could affect the ability of the Marine Corps to sustain current manpower levels is the impact of unemployment. Though most indicators suggest that recent high unemployment rates have positively affected recruiting rates, the relationship between the two is uncertain.

Indeed, little is known about how and why American youth volunteer for military service at different times and in different circumstances—how, for example, advertising, choice of assignment, educational benefits, and the like, affect their decisions. The fact that the services met their quantitative goals even before high unemployment levels were reached suggests that if growing unemployment had any effects, it increased the number of prospective volunteers and hence enabled the services to be more selective in their recruitment. Thus it is safe to conclude that the Marines are currently attracting the best quality mix possible under present pay comparability standards and recruitment policies. Conversely, if the nation moves back toward fuller employment levels it is likely that the quality of Marine Corps recruits will deteriorate.

If a sufficient number of volunteers meeting established standards of quality and representation cannot be recruited, pressures to renew conscription or to offer additional incentives will mount. Within limits, a third possibility exists: smaller military forces. Reducing the size of the Marine Corps would increase the probability that an elite corps of Marine volunteers could be attracted without returning to the draft or without increasing monetary incentives.

(because they are institutionalized or unqualified for military service with mental, physical, or moral limitations, and those already in the service) and those who are *not likely* to volunteer (because they are full-time college students who have not dropped out of school in their first or second year and who are not veterans). (For the methodology of this approach, see Martin Binkin and John D. Johnston, *All-Volunteer Armed Forces: Progress, Problems, and Prospects*, Report prepared for the Senate Committee on Armed Services, 93:1 [GPO, 1973].)

16. In July 1975, the Marine Corps announced discontinuance of the two-year enlistments in favor of three- and four-year enlistments. As a result, the average duration of the first-term enlistment will increase and thus reduce turnover. Over the long term, an increase of three months in the average duration of enlistment would lead to a decrease of about 7 percent in annual recruitment requirements.

CHAPTER SEVEN

WHERE DOES THE MARINE CORPS GO FROM HERE? RECOMMENDATIONS AND ALTERNATIVES

For America's most honored fighting force, justifiably proud of its past, this is a time for choice. In an era of shrinking prospects for direct U.S. military intervention abroad the need for the Corps' principal mission—amphibious warfare—is less apparent than in the past. Moreover, Marine divisions lack the firepower and mobility required for war against this nation's most powerful and likely adversaries. The United States Marine Corps, in short, is well suited for amphibious operations in the third world, where U.S. intervention now seems increasingly unlikely, and less well suited for combat in the key areas—Europe, Northeast Asia, and the Middle East—to whose security U.S. policy now assigns highest priority and against which technologically advanced opponents are likely to be deployed.

Within the Corps, the competition between flyers and foot soldiers for resources is increasing. Marine aviation now consumes more than half of each dollar spent on the Corps. The result is a widening imbalance between Marine air power, which is geared for the most sophisticated kind of combat and Marine infantry, whose fighting prowess still depends on the physical stamina of the footslogging rifleman.

And to add to these dilemmas, the Marine Corps is experiencing an embarrassing growth in disciplinary problems that jeopardizes the elite reputation of which it, and the nation, are rightly so proud.

Recommendations

So where does the Marine Corps go from here? It cannot remain as it is, structured for past rather than likely future international contingencies. As a result of our examination of the Corps and the major challenges it faces, we make the following general recommendations. They are departures from the present USMC posture that we believe should be undertaken regardless of the role assigned to the Corps or its possible size.

Only four Marine regiments and associated air units (equivalent to one and one-third Marine Amphibious Forces) should be structured principally for amphibious warfare. We base our recommendation on the following: (1) The growing constraints upon U.S. exercise of the amphibious "option" discussed in chapter 4. Since 1945, the Marine Corps has not conducted an amphibious assault or training exercise involving more than one Marine Amphibious Force. (2) The lack of available amphibious shipping to lift more than one and one-third MAFs simultaneously. These two factors together impose a ceiling on the size of amphibious forces. But (3) one and one-third MAFs is also a floor because it is the smallest force that can sustain the present number of battalion landing teams afloat without paying a stiff price in personnel turbulence or indiscipline. We support the continual deployment of four BLTs as an effective hedge against future amphibious contingencies. Yet only two BLTs—one in training and one undergoing reconstitution—are necessary to sustain one BLT afloat. This two-to-one ratio is the same as that used by the Navy in sizing its carrier task forces. Thus a force of one and one-third MAFs (twelve battalions) could support present peacetime deployments.

The present geographical deployment of BLTs should be altered by transferring one BLT from the Pacific to the Mediterranean. The combination of diminishing U.S. ground force requirements in Asia and the continuing credibility of limited amphibious contingencies in the Middle East, we believe, justifies reducing Marine BLTs in the Pacific from two to one and increasing the number in the Mediterranean from one to two. The intermittent deployment of a BLT in the Caribbean would remain unchanged. Thus the proposed redistribution of BLTs would be as follows:

	Pacific	*Mediterranean*	*Caribbean*
Present	2	1	1
Proposed	1	2	1

The present level of Marine Corps investment in tactical aviation should be sharply reduced. The principal opportunity cost of allocating to fixed-wing tactical aircraft some 45 percent of the total spending attributable to the Corps has been to deny USMC ground forces the organic firepower and cross-country mobility needed for more demanding contingencies. We have discovered no convincing rationale for equipping the Marines with aircraft, such as the F-4 or A-6, that are designed mainly for air superiority and interdiction. The U.S. Air Force or carrier-based naval aircraft can fulfill these missions for the Marine Corps as they have for the Army. Phasing out such aircraft, which now cost the Corps close to $700 million a year to operate, would not only release funds for modernizing Marine ground components but also allow Marine aviation to focus exclusively upon close air support. Thus we recommend the elimination of seventeen tactical air squadrons and their associated manpower, estimated at about 29,000 personnel, or 45 percent of the total now attributable to Marine aviation. We consider the remaining tactical fixed-wing forces—five A-4 and three AV-8 squadrons—sufficient to provide organic close air support for Marine ground forces in amphibious operations.

Most of the Fourth MAF (Reserve) should be disbanded. We see no continuing need for maintaining a *full* Marine division-wing team in reserve status. It would take four or five months to mobilize and deploy the Fourth MAF; and, in any event, we see no foreseeable contingency or set of contingencies that would require the commitment of four Marine divisions. Therefore, we conclude that the Fourth MAF can and should be dismantled except perhaps for (1) selected subunits to be maintained as affiliated reserve components of active formations, and (2) selected individuals retained as wartime fillers for active units that are presently under strength.

Even if the Marine Corps were to remain configured principally for amphibious operations, its capacity to carry out such operations would not be jeopardized by either the loss of its F-4 and A-6 squadrons or the disbandment of the Fourth MAF. These two measures can be justified on efficiency grounds alone and should be undertaken regardless of the posture adopted by the Corps in the future.

Four Alternative Postures

If our above recommendations—retaining one and one-third MAFs for amphibious operations, transferring one BLT from the Pacific to the Mediterranean, eliminating the F-4 and A-6 squadrons, and disbanding most of the Fourth MAF—are accepted, then what should be done with the Marine forces in excess of those deemed necessary for the amphibious mission? We present four alternative postures, together with their respective cost and structural implications, and assess the broader consequences of each for U.S. general purpose forces.[1]

1. The reader is cautioned against viewing the *specific* alternatives presented here as recommendations. Our purpose is simply to identify possible future directions of the

Each of the alternatives poses a different answer to the question of what to do with one and two-thirds Marine divisions and their associated air units that are not assigned to the amphibious mission. Each alternative assumes that our general recommendations are adopted. The *first* alternative would simply reduce the Corps to an amphibious assault force of one and one-third divisions and associated helicopter and close air support. The *second* would transfer to the Corps the primary responsibility for sustained inland combat in Asia, a responsibility now borne mainly by the Army's 2nd and 25th Infantry Divisions in Korea and Hawaii. The *third* would make the USMC the sole repository of U.S. quick-reaction capabilities by creating a Marine airborne division in place of the Army's 82nd Airborne Division. And the *fourth* would gear the Corps for combat in Central Europe.

In all four alternatives, the one and one-third MAFs retained for the amphibious mission would be constituted as follows:

The Second MAF at Camp Lejeune, North Carolina, and one regiment of the First MAF now at Camp Pendleton, California, would be retained for amphibious operations worldwide, supported by five A-4 and three AV-8 squadrons. Four BLTs would continue to be deployed afloat. Two in the Mediterranean and one intermittently in the Caribbean would be attached to the Second MAF. One Marine Amphibious Brigade, which would be located in Hawaii, would support the single BLT afloat in the Pacific.

In line with our general recommendations none of the alternatives envisions completely eliminating the USMC or expanding the Corps beyond its present size. The case for the former option might rest upon the judgment that the Corps is little more than a redundant army and tactical air force—that is to say, that all of the USMC's present missions could be effectively shouldered by the other services. We believe that the Marines, who represent almost one-fifth of America's ground forces, have an important contribution to make to the nation's security. Doing away with the Corps would be politically infeasible in any event. The argument for *larger* Marine forces might be based either on an assumption that total U.S. ground forces should be increased beyond nineteen active divisions cur-

Marine Corps and to illustrate how various perspectives on the issues explored in the preceding analysis could affect the cost and configuration of the Corps. It is left to the reader to determine, based on his own perspective, which if any of the alternatives he would prefer. Also, no precision is claimed for the cost estimates given here. The method of allocating indirect costs, which is explained in table 7-3, note b, is an attempt to simplify a complex and poorly defined relationship, and it has inherent limitations.

Table 7-1. U.S. Marine Corps Ground Force Structure: Current (1975) and Proposed under Four Alternatives, by Types of Maneuver Battalions Assigned to Active Divisions

	Types of maneuver battalions						
Divisions	*Amphibious infantry*[a]	*Infantry*	*Mechanized*	*Armored*	*Armored cavalry*	*Air cavalry*	*Total*
Current (1975)							
1st Division	9	...	...	...	...	...	9
2nd Division	9	...	...	...	...	...	9
3rd Division	9	...	...	...	...	...	9
Total	27	...	...	...	...	...	27
Alternative One							
1st Division	3	...	...	...	...	...	3
2nd Division	9	...	...	...	...	...	9
3rd Division	[b]	...	...	...	...	...	...
Total	12	...	...	...	...	...	12
Alternative Two							
1st Division	3[c]	3	1	1[d]	...	1[d]	9
2nd Division	9	...	...	...	...	...	9
3rd Division	...	6	1	1[d]	...	1[d]	9
Total	12	9	2	2	...	2	27
Alternative Three							
1st Division	3[e]	8[f]	...	1	...	1[g]	13
2nd Division	9	...	...	...	...	...	9
3rd Division	[b]	...	...	...	...	...	...
Total	12	8	...	1	...	1	22[h]
Alternative Four							
1st Division[i]	3[e]	...	6	4	1	...	14
2nd Division	9	...	...	...	...	...	9
3rd Division[i]	...	...	6	4	1	...	11
Total	12	...	12	8	2	...	34[j]

Sources: Current (1975) data supplied by the Department of the Army, July 1975; Alternatives One, Two, Three, and Four, authors' estimates.

a. Infantry battalions trained and equipped principally for amphibious assault.

b. Disbanded.

c. These three battalions would form an independent regiment attached to the First Division. Thus under Alternative Two, the nonamphibious portion of the First Division would consist of six active and three reserve maneuver battalions.

d. Obtained from USMC force troops.

e. The three battalions and requisite air support in the First Division would form an independent regiment stationed in Hawaii. Thus under Alternative Three, the First Marine Division would actually contain a total of ten active nonamphibious maneuver battalions.

f. Equivalent in manpower to six Marine infantry battalions as currently configured.

g. Created from the helicopter group of the disbanded Third MAF.

h. Equivalent to twenty Marine infantry battalions as currently configured.

i. The manpower in the eleven nonamphibious battalions is equivalent in manpower to seven and one-half Marine infantry battalions as currently configured.

j. Equivalent in manpower to twenty-seven Marine infantry battalions as currently configured.

rently planned or on the conclusion that the Marines should constitute a larger part of a nineteen-division force. Neither case is given serious consideration since an expansion of Marine Corps strength beyond 200,000 would, in our view, exacerbate the already serious disciplinary problems besetting the Corps. Any increase in Corps manning would be impractical as long as it must rely on recruitment by voluntary means.

The reader's choice in the final analysis will be shaped by his or her perceptions of the appropriate size and structure of U.S. conventional forces and the role of the Marine Corps as a component of those forces. How the proposed alternatives affect the structure of the Corps' ground combat forces is shown in table 7-1.

Alternative One: Eliminating One and Two-thirds MAFs

Under this alternative, the Marine Corps would be reduced to one and one-third Marine Amphibious Forces geared exclusively for amphibious warfare. The Corps' remaining one and two-thirds division-wing teams (the Third MAF and two regiments of the First MAF) would be demobilized, together with the Fourth (Reserve) MAF.

Implications for the Marine Corps

The demobilization of one and two-thirds MAFs would reduce the size of the Corps from the present 196,000 personnel to approximately 111,700.[2] Such a drastic contraction would be hotly opposed by the Marine Corps for obvious reasons, not the least of which is that it would transform the Corps from what is now essentially a separate service into an appendage of the Navy, with all the attendant loss of bureaucratic clout.

Implications for U.S. General Purpose Force Posture

As shown in table 7-2, realization of Alternative One would have a significant impact on overall U.S. ground force posture. Elimination of one and two-thirds MAFs would reduce total active U.S. ground forces projected for fiscal 1977 from nineteen divisions to seventeen and one-third

2. Although Marine force structure would be reduced by over one-half, neither costs nor manpower would diminish proportionately. The principal reason for this is the fixed cost component of supporting units. For example, the number of personnel assigned to Headquarters, USMC, is relatively insensitive to changes in combat manpower.

Table 7-2. Size and Geographical Orientation of U.S. Army and Marine Corps Forces: Projected for Fiscal Year 1977 and Proposed under Alternative One

Structure and orientation	*1977*	*Alternative One*
USMC active personnel	196,000	111,700
Ground forces	131,000	75,700[a]
Aviation forces	65,000	36,000[b]
Army active personnel	785,000	785,000
Number of divisions	19	17⅓
USMC	3	1⅓
Army	16	16
Number of maneuver battalions[c]	193	178
Geographical orientation[d]		
Asia/Pacific	51[e]	36
Europe	111[f]	111
Other	31[g]	31

Sources: Fiscal 1977 figures, authors' estimates based on information from *Annual Defense Department Report, FY 1976 and 197T*, Report of Secretary of Defense James R. Schlesinger to the Congress on the FY 1976 and Transition Budgets, FY 1977 Authorization Request and FY 1976–1980 Defense Programs (February 5, 1975); Department of Defense, "Manpower Requirements Report for FY 1976," prepared by the Department of Defense, Office of the Assistant Secretary for Manpower and Reserve Affairs (February 1975; processed).

a. Reduction includes personnel assigned to ground combat and support units associated with one and two-thirds divisions, and a proportionate share of personnel in indirect support units (assuming one-half of the manpower assigned to such units is variable).

b. Reduction includes personnel assigned to helicopter squadrons associated with one and two-thirds MAFs, all assigned to F-4 and A-6 squadrons, and support personnel attributable to each.

c. Only those battalions in divisions.

d. Based on location, type, and where possible, stated mission of parent division.

e. Maneuver battalions in the 1st and 3rd Marine Divisions, and the Army's 2nd, 9th, 25th, and 7th Infantry Divisions.

f. Maneuver battalions in the Second Marine Division and in all of the Army's five mechanized and four armored (including the First Cavalry) divisions.

g. Maneuver battalions in divisions that are not considered oriented toward contingencies in a particular geographic region—the Army's 24th Infantry, 82nd Airborne, and 101st Airmobile Divisions.

divisions. This reduction, however, would affect only forces that are structured primarily for contingencies in Asia and the western Pacific. Essentially light infantry formations, Marine divisions are not, as indicated above, optimally configured for the high-intensity combat environments of Europe or the Middle East; it is no coincidence that the First and Third MAFs, whose demobilization is called for in this alternative, are deployed in the Pacific region. Thus Alternative One would not affect current U.S. capacity to respond to contingencies outside Asia.

Alternative One obviously would be attractive to those who believe that present U.S. forces oriented toward Asia are excessive in view of declining U.S. commitments in that area and the growing odds against future U.S. combat involvement there. Substantial forces for Asia would still be retained: three Army divisions—the 2nd in Korea, the 25th in Hawaii, and the 9th at Fort Lewis, Washington—and, if necessary, new Army divisions could be created mainly for combat in that region, such as the 7th Infantry Division now being formed at Ford Ord, California.

On the other hand, a Marine Corps of one and one-third MAFs—the bulk of it geared for transatlantic contingencies—would not provide an effective hedge against an unexpectedly large conflict in Asia. In the event of another "Korea" or "Vietnam," large USMC contingents would not be available, as they were in both of those conflicts, as a major repository of additional ground combat forces outside the Army. Thus the viability of Alternative One hinges upon the validity of the assumption of a declining U.S. force requirement in Asia; that is, the improbability of another Korea or Vietnam.

Budgetary Consequences

The elimination of one and two-thirds active MAFs and one reserve MAF would substantially reduce the budget. As table 7-3 shows, average annual savings would be close to $2 billion after one-time costs of approximately $180 million.

Table 7-3. Summary of Proposed Force Changes and Estimated Financial Implications, Alternative One

Millions of fiscal 1976 dollars

Modification	*One-time cost*[a]	*Annual saving (−)*
Deactivate one and two-thirds active divisions and associated support[b]	100	−985
Deactivate twelve F-4 and five A-6 squadrons[c]	70	−880
Disband Marine Reserve Division-Wing[d]	10	−120
Net cost or saving	180	−1,985

Source: Authors' estimates.

a. One-time costs are involved in making any force changes. For example, when units are disbanded, facilities must be shut down, units must be transferred, and in some cases, personnel must be laid off. These costs, which vary widely depending on the rules and speed of deactivation, are difficult to estimate with precision. A rough rule of thumb, used throughout the study, assumes that, on the average, one-time costs associated with disbanding units would be equal to 10 percent of the annual cost of operating those units.

b. Includes costs associated with ground units consisting of one and two-thirds divisions and a proportionate share of "variable" direct and indirect support costs. There is little agreement among analysts as to the ratio of "variable" to "fixed" costs in support functions. In some instances, the activity is almost completely insensitive to changes in force or manpower levels (for example, research and development and intelligence programs). In other cases, a large portion of the costs of an activity are variable (for example, maintenance and logistics). Moreover, the fixed-variable ratio depends on the magnitude of the reduction in forces. The number of people required to operate a base would be relatively insensitive to the deactivation, say, of a company or squadron. The elimination of a brigade or a division, on the other hand, could lead to complete closures of installations. For this alternative which calls for relatively large reductions, it has been assumed that all direct support costs (such as base operations) and one-half of indirect support costs (such as central supply and maintenance) are variable.

c. Includes annual direct cost of twelve F-4 and five A-6 squadrons and a proportionate share of direct and indirect support costs, assuming one-half of the latter is variable.

d. Includes Marine Corps Reserve operations and maintenance and personnel appropriations, and a share of Navy reserve operations and maintenance costs, which support Marine reserve aviation units.

Alternative Two: Replacing the Army in Asia

Under this alternative the Marine Corps would be assigned primary responsibility for sustained inland combat in Asia and the Pacific, a responsibility presently borne mainly by the Army. Marine ground formations would replace Army units currently deployed in that region, which could be either demobilized or restructured for contingencies elsewhere. Asia-oriented Army divisions stationed in the United States (such as the 9th Infantry Division at Fort Lewis, Washington) would be retained as a hedge against unusually demanding contingencies.

Specifically, the 3rd Marine Division, now headquartered in Okinawa, would replace the Army's 2nd Infantry Division in Korea, and the two regiments of the 1st Marine Division not assigned to amphibious operations would replace the Army's 25th Infantry Division in Hawaii, which presently contains only two active brigades. A helicopter capability would be retained by both Marine divisions; tactical fixed-wing support, however, would be provided by the Air Force and Navy. A regiment from the Marine Reserve Division would be designated as an affiliated reserve component of the brigade-short 1st Marine Division in much the same fashion as a reserve brigade rounds out the Army's 25th Division in Hawaii. Remaining components of the 4th Marine Division would be phased out and their personnel transferred to unpaid status in the Individual Ready Reserve. Two options would be open to the Army divisions now in the Pacific: demobilization (Option A), or reconfiguration for European contingencies (Option B).

Implications for the Marine Corps

The restructuring of five U.S. Marine regiments for sustained inland combat in Asia would entail only modest changes in force structure that could be accomplished at little cost. This mission would require preparation for combat (1) against infantry-heavy armies that are largely unmotorized and still comparatively unsophisticated technologically, and (2) in terrain that is likely to deny armored and tactical air forces a decisive influence on the outcome of hostilities. Such conditions, combining low-intensity but prolonged combat, characterized both the Korean and Indochinese conflicts.

The present structure, organization, and equipment of the Marine Corps is remarkably well suited for this Asian mission. As light infantry formations relying principally on artillery and plentiful quantities of tactical aviation for their fire support, Marine divisions have undertaken this mission successfully in the past, and there is every reason to expect that they could do so in the future.

Marine divisions are structurally similar to Army divisions oriented toward Asian and Pacific contingencies. Nevertheless, assignment of that mission to the 1st and 3rd Marine Divisions would call for the establishment in each division of at least one mechanized battalion, one armored battalion, and one air cavalry battalion (squadron) in order to provide the additional organic firepower, mobility, and armed reconnaissance capabilities necessary to carry out that mission.

The mechanized, armored, and air cavalry battalions, however, could be obtained by reconfiguring and retraining six of the eighteen infantry battalions in the 1st and 3rd Marine Divisions. Some equipment for these transformed battalions would be available from existing Marine assets. For example, the armored battalions could be obtained simply by transferring two of the three armored battalions in the Marine Corps' force troops.

In terms of maneuver battalions, these changes would result in the active Marine Corps force structure shown in table 7-1. Although none of the twenty-seven maneuver battalions in the Corps' three active divisions in 1975 would be eliminated, only twelve would remain configured principally for amphibious assault (as is the case for all four alternatives).

The formal assignment of the mission of sustained inland combat in Asia to the USMC would not relegate the Marines to simply an "Asia/Pacific" force; the Corps would continue to remain the sole repository of U.S. amphibious warfare capabilities, which although smaller (at least on paper) would nevertheless still be oriented toward contingencies worldwide. Under Alternative Two, however, the Marine Corps would have to accept the fact that amphibious assault was no longer its principal mission. Such an adjustment in present doctrinal focus could be difficult for Marines still infatuated with the great amphibious campaigns of World War II.

Implications for U.S. General Purpose Force Posture

The assumption by the Marine Corps of primary responsibility for sustained inland combat in Asia and the Pacific would have a significant impact on overall U.S. general purpose force posture. Option A would involve demobilization of the Army's two divisions (the 2nd and 25th)

Table 7-4. Size and Geographical Orientation of U.S. Army and Marine Corps Forces: Projected for Fiscal 1977 and Proposed under Alternative Two

		Alternative Two	
Structure and orientation	*1977*	*Option A*	*Option B*
USMC active personnel	196,000	175,100	175,100
Ground forces	131,000	131,000	131,000
Aviation forces	65,000	44,100	44,100
Army active personnel	785,000	718,000	785,000
Number of divisions	19	17	19
USMC	3	3	3
Army	16	14	16
Number of maneuver battalions[a]	193	177	193
Geographical orientation[b]			
Asia/Pacific	51[c]	35	35
Europe	111[d]	111	127
Other	31[e]	31	31

Sources: Same as table 7-2 and authors' estimates.
a. Only those battalions in divisions.
b. Based on location, type, and where possible, stated mission of parent division.
c. Maneuver battalions in the 1st and 3rd Marine Divisions, and the Army's 2nd, 9th, 25th, and 7th Infantry Divisions.
d. Maneuver battalions in the 2nd Marine Division and in all of the Army's five mechanized and four armored (including the First Cavalry) divisions.
e. Maneuver battalions in divisions that are not considered oriented toward contingencies in a particular geographic region—the Army's 24th Infantry, 82nd Airborne, and 101st Airmobile Divisions.

deployed in that region. The Army would then have fourteen divisions instead of the sixteen-division force projected for fiscal 1977. Although proposals for such a reduction are not likely to be warmly received by the Army, it has been argued that U.S. ground forces presently configured for combat in Asia could be substantially cut without jeopardizing remaining important U.S. interests in that region.[3]

Divisions currently geared for Asian contingencies include the 1st and 3rd Marine Divisions and the Army's 2nd, 25th, 9th, and 7th (at Fort Ord, California) infantry divisions—one-third of all U.S. divisions. Together these six divisions, as shown in table 7-4, contain over 26 percent of the total number of maneuver battalions in active U.S. Marine and Army divisions projected for fiscal 1977. The Army's comparatively light 82nd Airborne and 101st Air Assault Divisions (possessing an aggregate of twenty-one maneuver battalions) also are eminently suited for Asian contingencies.

The disposition of the 2nd and 25th Divisions, however, hinges on how

3. See, for example, Barry M. Blechman, Edward M. Gramlich, and Robert W. Hartman, *Setting National Priorities: The 1976 Budget* (Brookings Institution, 1975), chap. 4.

the recent growth in Soviet military capabilities has affected the military balance in Europe. Some believe that increasing the size of U.S. ground forces trained for European contingencies is necessary to counter the growing asymmetries in the relative size of NATO and Warsaw Pact forces and in the differing emphasis that is placed on the initial intensity and duration of combat operations. To those who hold this view, Option B—returning the 2nd and 25th Divisions to the continental United States and reconfiguring them for European contingencies—obviously would be attractive.

On the other hand, demobilization of these divisions would be welcomed by those who feel that an increase in U.S. force levels in Europe is less significant than the way in which those forces are organized and deployed. Those who subscribe to the so-called short war school of future conflict in Europe argue that forces currently earmarked for NATO are already numerically sufficient; more important, in their opinion, are improvements in the combat-to-support ratio of U.S. forces in Europe and reduction in the time that it takes to redeploy U.S. divisions from the United States to Europe. Even if present proposals to strengthen U.S. strategic airlift capability are approved, they have argued, it is doubtful that two additional divisions could be sent to Europe in sufficient time to influence the outcome of a conflict of the comparatively short duration envisaged.

Alternative Two also would reduce the number of U.S. maneuver battalions that are dependent mainly upon marching for their mobility. By the close of fiscal 1977 unmechanized infantry battalions (including airborne infantry battalions) are expected to number seventy-five, or almost 40 percent of all maneuver battalions within divisions. Under Alternative Two, the number of "straight-legged" battalions would be reduced to sixty-five, or 37 percent of the total under Option A, and some 34 percent of the total under Option B.

Budgetary Consequences

The financial implications of Alternative Two would vary markedly depending on whether or not the Army divisions were demobilized. Option A—removing the 2nd and 25th divisions from the Army structure—would yield annual savings of about $2 billion, after one-time costs of about $185 million associated with deactivation. Under Option B, which calls for keeping the divisions in the structure and reconfiguring them for European contingencies, average annual budgetary savings would amount to about $790 million. There would, however, be one-time costs of about $900 million to

Table 7-5. Summary of Proposed Force Changes and Estimated Financial Implications, Alternative Two

Millions of fiscal 1976 dollars

Modification and option	*One-time cost*	*Annual cost or saving (−)*
Marine Corps		
Deactivate twelve F-4 and five A-6 squadrons[a]	70	−880
Convert two battalions each to mechanized, armor, and air cavalry configurations[b]	70	10
Disband two Marine Corps reserve[c] regiments and associated air support	5	−60
Subtotal	145	−930
Army		
Option A: Deactivate 2nd and 25th Infantry Divisions and supporting elements	110	−1,120
Option B: Return 2nd and 25th Infantry Divisions to continental U.S. and reconfigure as mechanized divisions	755	140
Net cost or saving		
Option A[d]	185	−2,050
Option B	900	−790

Sources: Authors' estimates; Army costs based on data obtained from Office of the Comptroller of the Army, Directorate of Cost Analysis, "Army Force Planning Handbook" (June 1975, amended July 1975; processed).

a. Includes annual direct cost of twelve F-4 and five A-6 squadrons and a proportionate share of direct and indirect support costs, assuming one-half of the latter is variable.

b. For the most part, the additional cost would be associated with the procurement of weapons; to look like the Army mechanized battalion, for example, the Marines would have to buy 238 M-113 and 32 M-114 armored fighting vehicles, about 70 TOW launchers, as well as sizable numbers of helicopters for air cavalry squadrons. It is assumed that the Marines could form two tank battalions using existing Marine assets.

c. Includes Marine Corps reserve operations and maintenance and personnel appropriations, and a share of Navy reserve operations and maintenance costs, which support Marine reserve aviation units.

d. Under Option A, the one-time cost to reconfigure Marine units would be avoided since the equipment required for the Marine battalions would be available from demobilized Army divisions.

outfit the units with appropriate equipment and supplies. Table 7-5 summarizes the proposed force changes and their estimated financial implications.

Alternative Three: Taking On the Airborne Mission

Under Alternative Three the Marine Corps would become the sole repository of U.S. ground quick-reaction capabilities by assuming the responsibilities now shouldered by the Army's 82nd Airborne Division, which would be demobilized.

The 82nd Division is the Army's last remaining airborne formation. Because it is configured for airborne (parachute) operations, the 82nd is lightly equipped and can be quickly deployed by strategic airlift. Although large-scale combat airdrops are no longer feasible against a vigilant and sophisticated enemy,[4] the strategic and tactical mobility of airborne forces permits their rapid deployment to areas in which landing fields remain secure.

The 82nd Army division would be replaced by the six maneuver battalions not assigned to amphibious operations in the First MAF. They would be transformed into eight Army-sized airborne infantry battalions, which would form the core of a Marine airborne division.[5]

The present investment in airborne training facilities would be retained by basing the new division at Fort Bragg, North Carolina, the home of the 82nd Airborne Division. The base itself would be transferred to the Corps and members of the 82nd would be granted the option of joining the new division.

The Marine airborne division would receive a light armored battalion and an air cavalry battalion (squadron)—essential components of a division-sized airborne formation. The 3rd Marine Division and the Fourth MAF (Reserve) would be disbanded along with the 82nd Airborne Division. All Marine helicopter assets would be retained, but the 1st Marine Division would depend on Air Force and Navy for tactical fighter support.

Implications for the Corps

Like Alternative Two, Alternative Three would not require substantial or expensive changes in present Marine Corps force structure or equipment. Active Corps personnel, however, would be reduced by about 28 percent—from 196,000 to 142,000. Manpower for the armored and air cavalry battalions needed for the new Marine airborne division could be obtained

4. A combat airdrop is defined here as the parachuting of forces over territory that at the time of the drop is held by enemy troops. Historically, large combat drops have been almost uniformly unsuccessful against alert defenses. Failure has been due mainly to the inherent difficulty of (1) concentrating scattered landing forces in the face of hostile fire and (2) achieving a linkup with the main body of friendly forces moving forward from the battle line. A notable exception was the audacious German airborne assault on Crete in 1940; even in that operation, however, German parachute units sustained casualties of over 50 percent.

5. A Marine division nominally contains 17,784 personnel, compared to the 13,285 assigned to the Army's 82nd Airborne Division. A Marine infantry battalion nominally contains 1,110 personnel, substantially more than the 806 present in an Army airborne infantry battalion. Thus six Marine infantry battalions possess an aggregate of 6,660 personnel, almost equal to the total (6,848) in eight airborne battalions.

Table 7-6. Size and Geographical Orientation of U.S. Army and Marine Corps Forces: Projected for Fiscal 1977 and Proposed under Alternative Three

Structure and orientation	*1977*	*Alternative Three*
USMC active personnel	196,000	142,000
Ground forces	131,000	97,900
Aviation forces	65,000	44,100
Army active personnel	785,000	745,000
Number of divisions	19	17
USMC	3	2
Army	16	15
Number of maneuver battalions[a]	193	177
Geographical orientation[b]		
Asia/Pacific	51[c]	36
Europe	111[d]	111
Other	31[e]	30

Sources: Same as table 7-2 and authors' estimates.

a. Only those battalions in divisions.

b. Based on location, type, and where possible, stated mission of parent division.

c. Maneuver battalions in the 1st and 3rd Marine Divisions, and the Army's 2nd, 9th, 25th, and 7th Infantry Divisions.

d. Maneuver battalions in the 2nd Marine Division and in all of the Army's five mechanized and four armored (including the 1st Cavalry) divisions.

e. Maneuver battalions in divisions that are not considered oriented toward contingencies in a particular geographic region—the Army's 24th Infantry, 82nd Airborne, and 101st Airmobile Divisions.

Table 7-7. Summary of Proposed Force Changes and Estimated Financial Implications, Alternative Three

Millions of fiscal 1976 dollars

Modification	*One-time cost*	*Annual saving (−)*
Marine Corps		
Deactivate 3rd Marine Division and associated force troops[a]	40	−430
Deactivate twelve F-4 and five A-6 squadrons[b]	70	−880
Disband Marine Reserve Division-Wing[c]	10	−120
Subtotal	120	−1,430
Army		
Deactivate 82nd Airborne Division and associated initial supporting elements	50	−520
Net cost or saving	170	−1,950

Sources: Same as table 7-5 and authors' estimates.

a. Includes direct costs of the division and associated force troops, a proportional share of direct and indirect support costs, assuming one-half of the latter costs are fixed. Does not include the costs associated with helicopter aviation units, which would be retained.

b. Includes annual direct cost of twelve F-4 and five A-6 squadrons and a proportionate share of direct and indirect support costs, assuming one-half of the latter is variable.

c. Includes Marine Corps reserve operations and maintenance and personnel appropriations, and a share of Navy reserve operations and maintenance costs, which support Marine reserve aviation units.

by drawing personnel from the armored formations located in Marine Corps force troops, and from the helicopter group nominally assigned to the Third MAF. Equipment for these battalions would be available from the demobilized 82nd Airborne Division.[6]

In terms of maneuver battalions, these changes would result in the active Marine Corps force structure shown in table 7-1. The total number of maneuver battalions would be cut from the present twenty-seven to twenty-two, although the eight airborne infantry battalions would be equivalent in manpower to the six Marine infantry battalions in the 1st Division plus the new armored cavalry and air cavalry battalions.

Concentrating quick-reaction capabilities in a single service with few and relatively inexpensive changes in current structure and equipment are the advantages of Alternative Three. In addition, although it would entail the loss of one MAF, this proposal could not fail to enhance further the Marines' reputation as an elite force justifiably proud of its tradition of being "the first to fight."

Implications for U.S. General Purpose Force Posture

Demobilization of the Third MAF and the 82nd Airborne Division would yield a U.S. ground force of seventeen divisions (fifteen Army and two Marine) instead of the nineteen-division force projected for fiscal 1977. Alternative Three would not disturb present U.S. airborne capabilities; it would merely assign responsibility for maintaining them to the Marine Corps.

As shown in table 7-6, this alternative would considerably reduce both active ground force manpower and the portion of U.S. ground forces oriented principally to meet Asian contingencies. It would also cut down the number of unmechanized infantry battalions within divisions from a projected seventy-five to fifty-nine, or to some 33 percent of the total.

Budgetary Consequences

The effect of demobilizing the bulk of the Third Marine Amphibious Force and the Army's 82nd Airborne Division is shown in table 7-7. Average annual savings could top $1.9 billion following one-time costs associated with deactivation of about $170 million.

6. The Marine Corps' M-60 tanks are too heavy for employment in either airborne or airmobile operations. Under Alternative Three, however, the 82nd Airborne Division's M-551 Sheridan light tanks would be transferred to the Corps.

Alternative Four: Joining the Army in Europe

Under this alternative, the Marine Corps would be reoriented mainly toward sustained inland combat in Europe. The Corps would not replace but rather would "join" those Army forces already earmarked for NATO contingencies, preparation for which justifiably remains the principal determinant of the size and structure of U.S. general purpose forces. Specifically, the 3rd Division, now headquartered in Okinawa, and two regiments of the 1st Division (at Camp Pendleton) would move to the eastern United States. These fifteen battalions with 16,650 men (1,110 men in each battalion)—would be used to form twelve standard-sized mechanized battalions, eight armored battalions, and two armored cavalry battalions, containing an aggregate of 16,542 personnel (see table 7-1).[7] The new battalions would constitute the combat core of two Marine mechanized infantry divisions that, like the Army, would rely on the Air Force for fixed-wing tactical support.

Implications for the Marine Corps

The reconfiguration of five Marine regiments for sustained inland combat in Europe would entail profound and costly changes in present USMC force structure, doctrine, and deployment patterns. The twenty-two mechanized, armored, and armored cavalry battalions would be much more expensive to create and maintain than the airborne or standard infantry battalions contemplated under Alternatives Two and Three.

For example, the new battalions would require a total of about 430 main battle tanks, 840 armored personnel carriers, and over 800 other vehicles.[8] The aggregate "rollaway" cost (excluding initial spares and prorated research development, test, and evaluation costs) of just the tanks and the armored personnel carriers would be approximately $319 million in fiscal

7. The nominal strengths of Army mechanized, armored, and armored cavalry battalions are 848, 554, and 967 personnel, respectively. Thus $(12 \times 848) + (8 \times 554) + (2 \times 967) = 16{,}542$.

8. The calculations are as follows: 54 tanks for each of the 8 armored battalions, amounting to 432 tanks. Sixty armored personnel carriers for each of the 12 mechanized battalions, 9 each for the 8 armored battalions, 25 each for the 2 armored cavalry battalions, amounting to 842 armored personnel carriers. Other tracked vehicles (cargo and mortar carriers; command, reconnaissance, and recovery vehicles) would be allocated as follows: 35 each for the 12 mechanized battalions, 26 each for the 8 armored battalions, and 92 each for the 2 armored cavalry battalions, reaching a total of 812 tracked vehicles.

1975 dollars.[9] Large numbers of additional tracked vehicles, to say nothing of thousands of soft-wheeled vehicles, would be required (1) for units such as the support command and division artillery that are located in each division base, and (2) to provide an adequate maintenance float.

Most of these and other major items or equipment would be obtainable only from current production because they cannot be supplied from the Marine Corps inventory, either at all or in sufficient quantity. No equipment would be available from the Army, as in other alternatives, since under Alternative Four no Army units would be demobilized. For example, the USMC's current inventory of about 450 tanks—even though it is being modernized by the introduction of M-60s—is woefully inadequate for two mechanized divisions and their combined maintenance float requirements. As for the armored personnel carriers, the Corps' relative handful of LVT-P7 amphibious assault vehicles are ill suited for combat in Europe, certainly compared to the Army's M-113 and the planned mechanized infantry combat vehicle (MICV). Preparation for NATO contingencies also would require procurement of greater quantities of TOW and Dragon antitank missiles than the number currently projected for fiscal 1977.

The wrenching implications of Alternative Four would not be confined solely to force structure and deployment patterns. The Marine Corps also would have to undertake a profound doctrinal reorientation. Preparation for combat in the European theater would require a doctrine suited for a technologically sophisticated battlefield environment characterized by high-speed armored operations and intense levels of violence. Indeed, realization of Alternative Four would strike at the very heart of the Corps' self-perception. The footslogging, self-reliant infantryman could no longer be regarded as the mainstay of its operations. At least in Europe, the Marines would have to acknowledge the inherent superiority of formations in which groups of more interdependent soldiers are encased in protective, highly mobile, hard-hitting armored fighting vehicles. Nor could the Corps any longer claim to be elite when its main justification would be to provide additional ground troops for U.S. forces already configured for NATO contingencies. The Marine Corps would inevitably play second fiddle to the Army. And the Marines' reputation for austerity—as well as pride in it—could not survive the logistic requirements of mechanization.

9. Based on a unit cost of $588,000 for the M-60A1 tanks and $78,000 for the M-113A1 armored personnel carrier. (*Department of Defense Budget for Fiscal Year 1976: Program Acquisition Costs by Weapons System* [Department of Defense, 1975], pp. 68–69.)

Table 7-8. Size and Geographical Orientation of U.S. Army and Marine Corps Forces: Projected for Fiscal 1977 and Proposed under Alternative Four

Structure and orientation	*1977*	*Alternative Four*
USMC active personnel	196,000	175,100
Ground forces	131,000	131,000
Aviation forces	65,000	44,100
Army active personnel	785,000	785,000
Number of divisions	19	19
USMC	3	3
Army	16	16
Number of maneuver battalions[a]	193	200
Geographical orientation[b]		
Asia/Pacific	51[c]	36
Europe	111[d]	133
Other	31[e]	31

Sources: Same as table 7-2 and authors' estimates.
a. Only those battalions in divisions.
b. Based on location, type, and where possible, stated mission of parent division.
c. Maneuver battalions in the 1st and 3rd Marine Divisions, and the Army's 2nd, 9th, 25th, and 7th Infantry Divisions.
d. Maneuver battalions in the 2nd Marine Division and in all of the Army's five mechanized and four armored (including the 1st Cavalry) divisions.
e. Maneuver battalions in divisions that are not considered oriented toward contingencies in a particular geographic region—the Army's 24th Infantry, 82nd Airborne, and 101st Airmobile Divisions.

Implications for U.S. General Purpose Forces

The two principal consequences of Alternative Four for overall U.S. general purpose force posture would be (1) a dramatically enhanced ground force orientation toward European contingencies, and (2) an equally sharp contraction of unmechanized infantry formations. As shown in table 7-8, two-thirds of all maneuver battalions within divisions would be oriented principally toward Europe, compared to only about 57 percent currently projected for fiscal 1977. U.S. ground force posture under Alternative Four therefore would be much more in line with the planning assumption of the primacy of the European contingencies than is presently the case. Maneuver battalions geared to Asian contingencies would decline from a projected 26 percent of the total to only 18 percent.

The impact of Alternative Four on the structure of U.S. ground forces is shown in table 7-9. Unmechanized infantry battalions within the Marine Corps' three divisions and the Army's projected sixteen divisions will by fiscal 1977 account for almost 40 percent of all maneuver battalions within divisions. Many analysts believe that such a high proportion of foot soldiers in a ground force presumably geared mainly for the most technologically demanding of contingencies is inconsistent. Under Alternative Four (as in Option A of Alternative Two) unmechanized infantry battalions

Table 7-9. U.S. Ground Force Structure, by Types of Maneuver Battalions within Divisions: Projected for Fiscal 1977 and Proposed under Alternative Four

	1977		*Alternative Four*	
Type of battalion	*Number*	*Percent*	*Number*	*Percent*
Unmechanized infantry[a]	75	39	60	30
Mechanized infantry	50	26	62	31
Armored	52	27	60	30
Other[b]	16	8	18	9
Total	193	100	200	100

Sources: Same as table 7-2 and authors' estimates.
a. Includes airborne infantry battalions.
b. Armored cavalry and air cavalry battalions.

would shrink to only about 30 percent of the total. Moreover, armored and mechanized battalions—the core of any credible ground combat force in NATO—would increase from 53 to 61 percent of all battalions.

Budgetary Consequences

The reconfiguration of one and two-thirds USMC divisions for sustained inland combat in Europe would entail major initial costs. As shown in table 7-10, about $900 million in one-time costs would be needed to convert five Marine regiments into two mechanized divisions. Although the annual operating costs of these divisions would increase by about $260 million, net annual operating costs would decrease by about $740 million because of the reduction in outlays for Marine air power.

Table 7-10. Summary of Proposed Force Changes and Estimated Financial Implications Alternative Four
Millions of fiscal 1976 dollars

Modification	*One-time cost*	*Annual cost or saving (−)*
Marine Corps		
Convert five Marine regiments into two mechanized divisions and increase force troops accordingly[a]	830	+260
Deactivate twelve F-4 and five A-6 squadrons[b]	70	−880
Disband Marine Reserve Division-Wing[c]	10	−120
Net cost or saving	910	−740

Sources: Same as table 7-5 and authors' estimates.
a. Based on the estimated incremental cost to create two mechanized divisions, each consisting of six mechanized battalions, four tank battalions, and one air cavalry squadron. Initial costs associated with major procurement of weapons, including 270 M-60 tanks, 54 M-551 tanks, 928 M-113 and 352 M-114 armored personnel carriers and reconnaissance vehicles, sixty 155 mm and eight 8-inch guns, and eighty TOW launchers. These figures also include an additional quantity for war reserve stockpiles.
b. Includes annual direct cost of twelve F-4 and five A-6 squadrons and a proportionate share of direct and indirect support costs, assuming one-half of the latter is variable.
c. Includes Marine Corps reserve operations and maintenance and personnel appropriations, and a share of Navy reserve operations and maintenance costs, which support Marine reserve aviation units.

Table 7-11. Alternative Structures and Their Implications

Force level, manpower, cost or saving	Currently planned	Alternatives				
		(1) Eliminating $1\frac{2}{3}$ MAFs	(2) Replacing the Army in Asia		(3) Taking on the airborne mission	(4) Joining the Army in Europe
			Option A[a]	Option B[b]		
Marine Corps force levels						
Active divisions	3	$1\frac{1}{3}$	3	3	2	3
Active fighter and attack squadrons	25	8	8	8	8	8
Reserve division-wing teams	1	...	$\frac{1}{3}$	$\frac{1}{3}$	...	...
Army divisions	16	16	14	16	15	16
Manpower (thousands)						
Marine Corps	196	112	175	175	142	175
Army	785	785	718	785	745	785
Incremental cost or saving (−) (millions of fiscal 1976 dollars)						
One-time	...	180	185	900	170	910
Average annual	...	−1,985	−2,050	−790	−1,950	−740

Sources: Same as tables 7-2 and 7-5, and authors' estimates
a. Eliminating two Army divisions.
b. Reconfiguring two Army divisions.

In Conclusion

Four alternatives to current Marine Corps force posture and mission orientation have been presented in this chapter. Their basic characteristics and estimated budgetary consequences are summarized in table 7-11. In each alternative the Corps would retain a sizable amphibious assault capability. The first would demobilize remaining Corps forces. The second would restructure them for sustained inland combat in Asia, where they would replace Army units now deployed in that region. The Army units would either be disbanded or reconfigured for European contingencies. The third alternative would transfer to the USMC the entire responsibility for U.S. quick-reaction capabilities, whereas the fourth would add two Marine divisions to Army forces already earmarked for combat in Europe.

Those who believe that the era of direct, major U.S. military intervention in third world conflicts is at an end and therefore that U.S. ground forces oriented toward contingencies in developing countries could be reduced will find Alternatives One, Two (Option A), and Three attractive. Remaining U.S. forces would be adequate to fulfill U.S. commitments to Europe and Japan. Alternatives Two (Option B) and Four, on the other hand, will appeal to those who believe that any further contraction of U.S. general purpose force levels would be misinterpreted by America's principal adversaries, and that any cuts in U.S. forces now slated for contingencies outside the NATO area should be balanced by an offsetting increase in forces designated for Europe. Those who favor centralizing all U.S. quick-reaction capabilities—whatever their magnitude—in one service will be attracted by Alternative Three.

Common to all four alternatives is a smaller Marine Corps in need of fewer volunteers and hence able to attract a higher proportion of qualified recruits than is now the case. A Corps of 112,000, as envisioned under Alternative One, would have little difficulty in obtaining volunteers from among the better qualified available applicants. Assuming continuation of recent recruiting experience, an annual enlistment of exclusively high school graduates scoring above the average on standardized tests would be within the realm of possibility. The reduction in annual recruitment that would stem from a Marine Corps consisting of 142,000 people, as called for in Alternative Three, should enable the Marine Corps to increase the proportion of new recruits possessing high school diplomas to well over 80 percent. Finally, under Alternative Two or Four, both of which would result in a

Corps of 175,000, Marine recruiters should have little difficulty meeting their announced objective: three of every four recruits a high school graduate. More important, the reduction in the number of aviation billets would enable Marine ground components to attract higher quality people.

THE FUTURE OF THE MARINE CORPS as an instrument of American military power will depend on a successful resolution of the issues raised in this study. Failure to do so could reduce that part of the Corps that cannot be justified on grounds of foreseeable amphibious operations to a costly anachronism increasingly haunted by its limitations. The Corps must shift its principal focus from seaborne assault to a more appropriate mission, such as garrisoning America's remaining outposts in Asia or defending Central Europe. The golden age of amphibious warfare is now the domain of historians, and the Marine Corps no longer needs a unique mission to justify its existence.

Types of Marine Aircraft

The types and functions of aircraft used in the United States Marine Corps are described below to amplify the discussions in chapters 3 and 5 of the current and possible future roles of Marine air power.

Attack Aircraft

There are three different types of aircraft whose main function is to support ground formations, from the initial assault through subsequent inland campaigns, by direct attacks on the enemy's engaged combat forces. These aircraft are the A-4 Skyhawk, the A-6 Intruder, and the AV-8 Harrier. In addition to this close air support role, squadrons equipped with these aircraft are trained to perform interdiction and escort missions.

The A-4, initially designed for the Navy as a simple, low-cost, lightweight attack aircraft, has been a workhorse for both the Navy and Marine Corps for the past two decades. The latest version, the A-4M, includes a more powerful engine than its predecessor, a drag chute and spoilers to facilitate short landings, and an additional armament capability. The aircraft is small, fast, highly maneuverable, and relatively easy to maintain; it carries a full range of ordnance including rockets, napalm, cluster bombs, and laser-guided weapons.

The A-6, a medium-weight, high-endurance, subsonic attack aircraft was designed mainly for all-weather attacks. Its avionic systems can locate strong radar targets without using ground-based navigational aids or control, and without ground visibility. It is capable of carrying a heavier and more varied ordnance load than earlier models of carrier-based attack aircraft; typically, it can carry thirty 500-pound bombs or three 2,000-pound bombs over long ranges. The aircraft in the A-6A series are being replaced by an updated model, A-6E, which is equipped with infrared sensors and a capability to deliver laser-guided weapons.

The AV-8 is the first vertical- or short-takeoff and landing (VSTOL) aircraft to be employed by any U.S. military service; it is particularly well suited to the amphibious mission. In contrast to the A-4 and A-6, which require carrier-length runways and catapults and arresting gear for seaborne operations, the Harrier can operate from amphibious lift ships. Since it requires no catapult or arresting gear, it can be based on amphibious assault (LPH) or large assault (LHA) vessels. Moreover, it can be sent ashore early in an operation and closely accompany the assault forces as they move inland. The Harrier has been criticized because of its limited range and payload. In a vertical- or short-takeoff mode, which would be required for most amphibious shipboard and initial beach pad operations, the AV-8 must pay a substantial penalty in range capability to carry ordnance. Its performance improves, however, with the takeoff distances that would be permitted when operating from a short airfield for tactical support (SATS)—a rapidly constructable airstrip consisting of short aluminum runways equipped, like carriers, with catapult and arresting gear.[1]

Future modernization plans for attack aircraft center on: (1) the continued procurement of A-4M aircraft—the twenty-four requested in the fiscal 1976 budget would enable the Corps to maintain A-4 force levels through 1981; (2) the equippage of the remaining A-6 squadrons with the improved A-6E version, and (3) the development of an advanced Harrier—called the AV-8 Plus that would eventually replace both the AV-8 and the A-4 fleets in the 1980s.

Fighter Aircraft

The mainstay of the Marine fighter aircraft fleet in recent years has been the F-4 Phantom. Although its primary role is to gain and maintain air superiority over the target area, it can also undertake attack missions. In-

1. The tradeoff between takeoff distance and performance can be illustrated as follows:

Takeoff roll (feet)	*Ordnance load (pounds)*	*Radius (nautical miles)*
Zero—vertical takeoff	3,000	50
600	5,000	125
1,500	8,000	222

(See Jeffrey L. Ethell, "The Flying Leathernecks," *Air International*, August 1975, p. 96.)

Table A-1. Nominal Fighter and Attack Component of a Marine Air Wing in Wartime, by Type and Number of Aircraft, Fiscal Year 1976

Aircraft type	*Primary mission*	*Number of squadrons*	*Unit equipment aircraft*	
			Per squadron	*Per wing*
Attack, AV-8 Harrier	Close air support	1	20	20
Attack, A-4 Skyhawk	Close air support	2	16	32
Fighter and attack, F-4 Phantom	Air superiority, interdiction, and close air support	4	15	60
All-weather attack, A-6 Intruder	All-weather close air support, and interdiction	2	12	24
Total		9	...	136

Source: Authors' estimates based on data appearing in USMC, Marine Corps Development and Education Command, *Fleet Marine Force Organization 1973* (Quantico, Va.: USMC Education Center, 1973).

deed, during the U.S. involvement in South Vietnam, where counterair missions were not required, Phantoms were used extensively in support of ground forces.

The selection of an aircraft to replace the F-4 has been a controversial issue for several years. Initial plans to equip the Marine Corps with updated F-4s gave way to a program under which four Marine squadrons were to receive F-14 aircraft. It appears, however, that the Marines will probably maintain twelve F-4 squadrons for the remainder of the decade. If the Department of Defense has its way, Marine F-4s will be replaced by F-18s, commencing in the early 1980s. The cost and design of the F-18 remains unclear, however, and procurement has not yet been approved either by the administration or Congress. Because of the complexity and the importance of this issue, it is discussed more fully in chapter 5.

In wartime, squadrons equipped with fighter and attack aircraft would be organized into air groups, three of which would be earmarked for each wing. The mix of fighter and attack aircraft assigned to a wing might be as shown in table A-1.

Other Aircraft

The Marine Corps has come to rely extensively on helicopters to transport forces from ship to shore during the assault phase of its amphibious operations and to provide both increased battlefield mobility and firepower as the campaign moves inland. The capacity to move men, equipment, and supplies by air is provided by three types of helicopters: the UH-1, CH-46, and CH-53.

The UH-1 is a lightweight utility helicopter used for a variety of support operations, including command and control, casualty evacuation, liaison and courier services, and search and rescue. The CH-46 medium helicopter is designed primarily for transporting troops; it can carry up to twenty-five fully equipped Marines or two tons of cargo. The CH-53D heavy helicopter, with the capability to carry about eight tons, can lift about 40 percent of a division's equipment, including the 155 mm towed howitzer.

The AH-1 Cobra attack helicopter mainly provides fire suppression support against light, mobile targets and is used as an armed escort for troop and cargo helicopters.

As shown in table A-2, a helicopter group in a wartime formation would probably consist of eight squadrons and would be attached to each air wing. The observation squadron, though not equipped with helicopters, is also attached to the helicopter group. It operates OV-10 aircraft to conduct aerial reconnaissance, observation, and forward air control activities. Rounding out the active Marine air forces is a composite reconnaissance squadron operating nine RF-4 aircraft, seven EA-6s, and an aerial refueling and transport squadron equipped with twelve KC-130 aircraft.

Substantial modernization of helicopter and reconnaissance aircraft is being undertaken. An improved attack helicopter (AH-1J), incorporating a threefold increase in ordnance payload capability, is to replace earlier models. Many of the new versions will have installed the TOW antiarmor missile system. Also under development is a follow-on to the CH-53 that

Table A-2. Nominal Composition of Marine Corps Helicopter Group in Wartime, by Type and Number of Helicopters and Fixed-Wing Aircraft

Type of squadron	*Aircraft type*	*Primary mission*	*Number of squadrons*	*Unit equipment aircraft*	
				Per squadron	*Per wing*
Light helicopter	UH-1	Utility support	1	21	21
Attack helicopter	AH-1	Close-in fire	1	18	18
Medium helicopter	CH-46	Personnel transport	3	18	54
Heavy helicopter	CH-53	Equipment and personnel transport	2	21	42
Observation	OV-10	Reconnaissance	1	12	12
Total			8	...	147

Source: Same as table A-1, p. 37.

will be able to take twice the payload of the earlier version. The CH-53E is being designed to lift all Marine tactical jet aircraft without disassembly, 90 percent of essential heavy combat equipment, and even another CH-53E. Finally, there are indications that the Marine Corps will soon push for procurement of a modern electronic countermeasure aircraft to replace the EA-6A aircraft, which it considers physically over age and approaching technological obsolescence.